Big Box Schools

Race and Education in the Twenty-First Century
Series Editors: Kenneth Fasching-Varner and Roland Mitchell

This series asks authors and editors to consider the role of race and education, addressing question such as "how do communities and educators alike take on issues of race in meaningful and authentic ways?" and "how education work to disrupt, resolve, and otherwise transform current racial realities?" The series pays close attention to the intersections of difference, recognizing that isolated conversations about race eclipse the dynamic nature of identity development that play out for race as it intersects with gender, sexuality, socio-economic class, and ability. It welcomes perspectives from across the entire spectrum of education from Pre-K through advanced graduate studies, and it invites work from a variety of disciplines, including counseling, psychology, higher education, curriculum theory, curriculum and instruction, and special education.

Titles in the Series

Big Box Schools: Race, Education, and the Danger of the Wal-Martization of Public Schools in America, by Lori Latrice Martin

Big Box Schools

*Race, Education, and the
Danger of the Wal-Martization of
Public Schools in America*

Lori Latrice Martin

LEXINGTON BOOKS
Lanham • Boulder • New York • London

Published by Lexington Books
An imprint of The Rowman & Littlefield Publishing Group, Inc.
4501 Forbes Boulevard, Suite 200, Lanham, Maryland 20706
www.rowman.com

Unit A, Whitacre Mews, 26-34 Stannary Street, London SE11 4AB

British Library Cataloguing in Publication Information Available

Library of Congress Cataloging-in-Publication Data

Martin, Lori Latrice.
Big box schools : race, education, and the danger of the Wal-martization of public schools in America / Lori Latrice Martin.
pages cm -- (Race and education in the twenty-first century)
Includes bibliographical references and index.
ISBN 978-1-4985-1041-7 (cloth : alk. paper) -- ISBN 978-1-4985-1042-4 (electronic)
1. Racism in education--United States. 2. Public schools--Economic aspects--United States. 3. Privatization in education--Social aspects--United States. 4. African Americans--United States--Social conditions. I. Title.
LC212.2.M38 2015
371.829'96073--dc23
2015007150

♾™ The paper used in this publication meets the minimum requirements of American National Standard for Information Sciences Permanence of Paper for Printed Library Materials, ANSI/NISO Z39.48-1992.

Printed in the United States of America

Constance Slaughter Harvey

Contents

Series Foreword

DuBuois some one hundred-plus years ago suggested that "the world problem of the twentieth century is the problem of the color line." Despite claims of a twenty-first-century evolution into a post-racial society, the reality of our times suggests that systemic oppression, marginalization, and alienation continue to play out along color lines. The Race and Education series asks authors and editors to consider "what is the role of race and education?," "how do communities and educators alike take on issues of race in meaningful and authentic ways?," and "how might education (from womb to tomb) work to disrupt, resolve, and otherwise transform current racial realities?"

While much scholarly attention has been paid to race over the last one hundred years very little substantive and systemic change seems to occur. Simultaneously in non-academic settings, the election of the nation's first president of color has prompted many to suggest that we have achieved racial nirvana—that the Obama-era has ushered in a post-racial reality. The vast majority of children of color continue to live in poverty, attend largely re-segregated public schools, are taught by pre-dominantly white teachers, and have little supported access to institutions of higher education. If we live in a post-racial moment, the highlights of those times include intensified segregation with little opportunity to openly dialogue about the realities, opportunities, and challenges of race. This series is a necessary addition to the literature because it works to understand race 1) through inter-disciplinary lenses, 2) draws on educational perspectives across the entire spectrum of education from Pre-K through advanced graduate studies, and 3) confronts the contributions between the articulation of being post-racial and the very racial realities of the times.

The Race and Education series covers a broad range of educational perspectives and contexts, drawing upon both qualitative/quantitative and em-

pirical/theoretical approaches to understanding race and education. Further
the series will contextualize the relationship between race and education not
just in the United States, but also in a variety of transnational settings. Disciplines such as counseling, psychology, higher education, curriculum theory,
curriculum and instruction, and special education all contribute to the larger
dialogue in the series. The series pays close attention to the intersections of
difference, recognizing that isolated conversations about race eclipse the
dynamic nature of identity development that play out for race as it intersects
with gender, sexuality, socio-economic class, and ability (among others).
Consequently, the series provides readers with multiple opportunities to examine the importance of race and education in both breadth and depth as it
plays out in the human experience.

*Big Box Schools: Race, Education, and the Danger of the Wal-Martiza-
tion of Public Schools in America* is the first book in a series of works that
will force all of us to take a hard look at educational reform efforts in
America and the impact said reforms have on historically disadvantaged
minority groups such as African Americans. Dr. Lori Latrice Martin, a sociologist at Louisiana State University, highlights the potential dangers contemporary educational polices present, particularly policies which are far
more concerned with profits than for people. Dr. Martin's work is not only
descriptive but also prescriptive. Dr. Martin's work not only identifies the
negative consequences associated with the adoption of a business model to
educational reform, but also examines grassroots efforts aimed at transforming schools while also empowering individuals, families, and communities.

—Kenneth Fasching-Varner and Roland Mitchell,
   Series Editors

Acknowledgments

Kenneth-Fasching-Varner, Roland Mitchell, Alissa Parra, Raymond Jetson, Chris Tyson, Stephen Finley, Joyce Jackson, LSU Dept of Sociology, Modrall Lathers, Kwando and Imani Kinshasa, Jannette Domingo, LSU Curriculum Theory Project, Mark Naison, Hayward Derrick Horton, Henry Louis Taylor, Emily and John Thornton, Lee and Edith Burns, Mahima Christian, Molly Quinn, Dione Footman, Lee Burns Jr., Walter Martin, Leroy Evans, Reggie and LaDonna Sanders, McKinley and Sue Johnson, Bill Batson, Frances Pratt, Alice Crowe Bell, Alicia Crowe, Willie and Goldie Bryant, Patricia Bullock, Mary White, Andre Sigmone, Angeline Butler, Dorothea Swann, Tifanie Pulley, Melinda Jackson, Shana Khan, Dari Green, David Rudder, Catherine H. Lowe, Derrick Martin Sr., Constance Slaughter-Burwell, James Burwell Sr., Derrick Martin Jr., James Burwell III, Sidney Rand, Larry Mathews, Ann Nash, Juanita Symister, Mark Chapman, Jasper and Ella Marsland, Everett Newton, Eugene and Myrtle Jones, Raymond Calimon, Ruth Case, Basil Smikle, Keith L. T. Wright, Shanille Mosely Thomas, David J. Leonard, Cheryl Ellis, Kelly Norman Ellis, Jeremiah Rogers, April Hawthorne, Jennifer Zeringue, Jourden Martin, Malcolm Joseph, Maurice Byrd, Corey Comier, Khadijah Thompson, Afi Paterson, Bianca Brown, Meagan Harrison, Kali Johnson, Sevetri Wilson, David Rudder, Sonya and Chris Williams, Maria Johnson, Zandria Law, Carissa Marcelle, Ashley MacKenzie, Nicolette Amstutz, and Emir Sykes.

Chapter One

Public Schools and Pathways to Prosperity

The American public school system is at a crossroad. We stand at a proverbial fork in the road deciding which pathway to take. One pathway is decorated with signs and institutions that will lead public education toward a destination of collective obligation, accountability, and responsibility that is student-centered, community-based, and driven by educators and parents working in the best interest of students, families, communities, and the broader society. The other pathway is littered with pamphlets, flyers, and electronic billboards falsely advertising the merits of school "choice." The direction American public schools appear to have taken over the past few decades is increasingly dotted with charter schools operated by for-profit multinational corporations (Mistler 2014), and themed public schools (Frankenberg and Siegel-Hawley 2008), which function as pseudo-private schools. These themed pseudo-private schools require students to apply to gain entry and maintain arbitrary grade point averages to avoid being sentenced to one-to-four years in their under resourced neighborhood schools (Strauss 2014).

The problems facing the American public school system are well documented, although not thoroughly understood. Signs the system is in peril are all around us. Racial differences in dropout rates are examples of one of the issues facing public education in America. Although the status dropout rates declined over the past few decades, according to the National Center for Education Statistics, the dropout rates for blacks were consistently higher than the dropout rates for whites (U.S. Department of Education 2013c).

In 1970, the percentage of individuals between the ages of sixteen and twenty-four who are not enrolled in school and have not earned either a diploma or General Educational Diploma was 15 percent. Over the next few decades the percentage of high school dropouts declined to 6.6 percent in

2012. The decline in high school dropout rates might be reason to celebrate if there were not documented evidence that far too many school districts were "cooking the books" and making their dropout rates appear lower than they are. The decline in the percentages of high school dropouts might also be reason to celebrate if the gap between whites and students of color were not so enduring. In 1970 the percentage of dropouts for all whites was 13.2 and nearly 28 for blacks. The percentage of dropouts for all males was about 14 in 1970, 12 for white males and almost 29 for black males. The percentage of female dropouts was even higher in 1970 than for males. In 1970 about 16 percent of females were high school dropouts. For white females about 14 percent were dropouts and for black females almost 27 percent were high school dropouts (U.S. Department of Education 2013c).

According to the U.S. Department of Education (2013c), by 1980 about 14 percent of sixteen- to twenty-four-year olds were dropouts. The percentage of white dropouts was 11.4, 19.1 for blacks, and 35.2 for Hispanics.

When it comes to gender differences, the percentage of male dropouts during that same year was 15.1 for all racial and ethnic groups. The percentage of white male dropouts was the lowest at 12.3 percent. The percentage of black male dropouts was 20.8 and the percentage of Hispanic male dropouts was 37.2. In the case of females between the ages of sixteen and twenty-four, the percentage of dropouts for all races was 13.1. White females had the lowest percentage of dropouts at 10.5 compared to 17.7 for black females and 33.2 percent for Hispanic females.

Fast forward to 2012, data from the U.S. Department of Education (2013c) shows that the percentage of dropouts in the U.S. was 6.6 percent. About 4 percent of whites were high school dropouts compared to 7.5 percent of blacks and 12.7 percent of Hispanics. When it comes to gender about 7 percent of all males were high school dropouts in 2012, but only 4.8 percent of white males were high school dropouts compared to 8 percent of black males and about 14 percent of Hispanic males. Nearly 6 percent of females were high school dropouts in 2012. A little less than 4 percent of white females were high school dropouts, while 7 percent of black females were high school dropouts and over 11 percent of Hispanic females were high school dropouts.

Some states are doing better than others (U.S. Department of Education 2013d) where graduation rates are concerned, but the graduation rates for some racial and gender groups are worthy of condemnation. The graduation rates for black males are well below 50 percent in many states. New York had the worse graduation rates for black males in the 2009–2010 cohort, followed by Washington, DC at 38 percent, and Iowa with a graduate rate for black males at 41 percent. Nebraska and Ohio round out the top five worse states for black male graduation rates. Only 44 percent of blacks males in Nebraska graduated in four years and just 45 percent of black males graduated in the 2009–2010 cohort in Ohio. In far too many states, including states with the highest black male enrollment, graduation rates are below 50 percent. Georgia, Florida, and New York have the second, third, and fourth highest black enrollment of all states in the U.S. and the graduation rates for black males in these states are 49, 47, and 37, respectively. In the ten states with the lowest black enrollment, the percentages of black male graduates ranges from 59 to 97 percent. In Maine, almost all of the black males graduated from high school; compare this statistic to Wyoming where only 59 percent of the black males graduated from high school.

For school districts with at least 10,000 black male students, the report from the U.S. Department of Education reveals that there are notable differences in graduate rates by race. In fact, a majority of the districts listed had graduate rates for black male students below 50%. Montgomery County, Maryland and Newark, New Jersey had the highest percentage of black male graduates at 74 percent. Rochester, New York had the lowest percentage of black male graduates at 9 percent. Detroit, Michigan; Clark County, Nevada; Philadelphia, PA; and Chatham County, Georgia round out the bottom five with graduation rates lower than 27 percent.

The linkages between dropout rates and other social issues are clear. The Center for Labor Market Studies at Northwestern University published a study which found that 10 percent of male high school dropouts are incarcerated or in detention. A quarter of black male high school dropouts are incarcerated (Weathersbee 2012).

Racial differences persist for black students who graduate from high school. Black high school graduates reported lower percentages of college enrollment in the year following high school graduation (U.S. Department of Education 2013d). In 2008, over 70 percent of white high school graduates were enrolled in college compared to 56 percent of black high school graduates.

Additionally, white high school dropouts have more wealth than black or Hispanic high school graduates. Clearly, the return on investment into education is not as great for many people of color when compared with whites. According to Bruenig's calculations of 2013 data from the Survey of Consumer Finances, white families with less than a high school education had a mean net worth of $161,500. The mean net worth for blacks with high school degrees was $162,800. Bruenig (2014) also shows that when we look at the median, which is relatively less susceptible to outliers, that the median net worth for whites with less than a high school education was about $51,000 compared to the median net worth of college educated black families which was about $26,000. Inequalities in wealth tell us much more about the cumulative effects of racial and ethnic inequality in America than inequalities in income (Martin 2013).

Aud, Fox, and Kewal-Ramani (2010) provide additional data on racial differences in education. In the report published in 2010, Aud et. al found that white students were concentrated in rural and suburban areas, while black students were concentrated in urban and suburban areas. The report also revealed that black students have a relatively higher chance of being held back a grade in both elementary school and in high school than white students. Twenty-one percent of black students were retained in a grade. Over 40 percent of black students in grades 6 through 12 were suspended from school, which was also higher than any other racial or ethnic group.

The number of black educators has declined over the years and the teaching profession has taken a hit in general. I analyzed census data to show the decline in the number of teachers of color in just the past few years. The results show an increase in the percentage of Asian and Hispanic teachers, but a decline in the percentage of black teachers, except in the case of special education teachers. In 2011, 14.5 percent of Pre-K and kindergarten teachers were black compared to 12.1 percent in 2013. The percentage of black elementary and middle school teachers decreased from 9.8 percent in 2011 to 9.4 percent in 2013. About 7 percent of secondary teachers were black in 2011 compared to 6.6 percent in 2013. Eight percent of special education teachers were black in 2011 and almost 10 percent of special education teachers were black in 2013.

The Harris Poll asks American's each year which occupations they considered most prestigious. In the 2006 Harris Poll, firefighters, scientists, doctors, and nurses were considered the most prestigious followed by teachers and military officers (Van Riber 2006). Over half of respondents said teachers have "very great prestige." The 2014 results saw the teaching profession drop from the top five and the percentage of Americans who said teachers have "very great prestige" also dropped. In the most recent year the questions was asked, the top five occupations with the greatest prestige, included: doctors, military officers, firefighters, scientists, and nurses (Griswold 2014). While 51 percent of respondents said teachers have "very great prestige" in 2006, only 21 percent said teachers have "very great prestige" in 2014. Additionally, teachers topped the list of professions respondents said had "not that much prestige" or "not at all prestigious." Teachers were tied with athletes for professions with the lowest levels of prestige in 2014, according to the Harris Poll (Griswold 2014). In 2006, only 10 percent of respondents thought teachers had "not that much prestige" and 0 percent of respondents thought being a teacher was "not at all prestigious" (Van Riber 2006). By 2014, 30 percent of respondents said teachers did not have much prestige and 10 percent said the profession was not at all prestigious (Griswold 2014). Not only is the teaching profession perceived less favorable today than in the past, but the doors to schools attended by majority black students are closing all too often.

During the 2010–2011 school year, almost 2,000 of the nation's nearly 200,000 schools closed. About 1,500 of the schools were regular schools. About 70 were special education schools and nearly 400 were alternative schools. The percentage of students enrolled in what the National Center for Education Statistics defines as school choice program has increased, especially for black students with devastating results (Liu and Taylor 2005). Over a fourteen-year period, the percentage of students attending a public school other than the assigned public school increased from 11 percent in 1993 to 16 percent in 2007. A higher percentage of black students attend choice programs than their white counterparts. Almost 40 percent of black students were enrolled in choice schools in 2007 compared to 20 percent of white students (U.S. Department of Education 2013a).

By the 2011–2012 school year, forty-two states passed legislation to establish charter schools. Alabama, Kentucky, Montana, Nebraska, North Dakota, South Dakota, Vermont, and West Virginia are the only states that have not passed a charter school legislation as of yet. Between the 1999–2000 school year and the 2011–2012 school year, the percentage of public schools that were charter schools increased from 1.7 percent to 5.8 percent. The total number of U.S. charter schools increased from 1,500 to 5,700.

The growth of pop-up schools, and other trends in public education, reveals the endurance of persistent racial inequality as well as persistent class inequality, and the intersection of both race and class. Those with the means, most of whom are white, have elected to abandon the public education system in areas where the majority of students are students of color, or where schools are changing from white to black.

What does the abandonment of the American public school system look like? I describe how it works in the following ways:

1. Whites leave the central city and create their own public school districts, which are predominantly affluent and white as a result of residential segregation (as distinct from self-segregation).
2. Whites take their students out of public schools and place them in private and parochial schools with tuition rates that often exceed the tuition at state universities.
3. Predominately white school districts and communities create an illusion of inclusion by offering a relatively small portion of economically disadvantaged students, and students of color, the opportunity to attend private and parochial schools, and at the same time divest in the public school system, where hundreds of thousands of children must remain.
4. Whites create public schools that are seemingly open to the general public, but charge tuition.

5. Members of the dominate racial group in America create pop-up programs within abandoned schools where the savage inequalities. Jonathan Kozol (1991) wrote about these highly visible inequalities in his book.
6. Members of the dominant racial group resort to blaming the victim instead of addressing the structural inequalities underpinning the entire educational system in America.

The right to a quality public education is one that fewer Americans are willing to fight for, especially when it comes to students of color. Instead of focusing on ways to address the issues facing public schools, efforts to further segregate schools by race and class are moving forward at lightning speed. The proliferation of what I call pop-up schools across the country, particularly in communities of color, is an example of the move away from traditional public schools.

Much like popular children's pop-up books, pop-up schools may be aesthetically pleasing, attractive at first glance, but in the wrong hands, are easily destroyed. In some instances, pop-up schools are schools that were designated as failing and closed down to prevent state takeovers. The so-called failing schools were then given new life, if not a new name, while retaining many of their problems, and devoid of programs and activities deemed as less important than test scores. Students in these pop-up schools (e.g., charter schools, magnet schools, gifted and talented programs) often lack access to the levels and types of resources readily available to more affluent and predominately white schools.

School administrators in pop-up schools have important, yet deceptive, roles to play. They are charged with selling a bill of goods to students, parents, teachers, and the community. The role of a school administrator is quite similar to the role of a used car salesperson. School administrators at these pop-up schools promise higher test scores and innovative pedagogical approaches. The frequent results, in reality, are new schools that have been hastily put together. The consequences are varied and quite severe.

Evidence that many schools are hastily put together and lacking in community support, include the absence of the basic infrastructure to handle tasks such as, scheduling, in-school tutoring for struggling students, and the advisement of extra-curriculum activities, which promote school spirit, enrich the overall academic experience and help students feel a sense of connectedness to their schools, their communities, and to their programs of study.

Pop-up schools are also plagued with a number of other issues. Jessie Ramey, a parent and historian at the University of Pittsburgh identified a number of persist problems in a critique of charter schools in Pennsylvania. Citing scholarly research, Ramey identified the following problems. Most charter schools are not producing better results on standardized exams than traditional public schools and many are spending less time on instruction. Many charter schools are hurting children by failing to provide them with experienced teachers and disciplinary policies that appear draconian. Ramey adds, charter schools are viewed as ideal places of investment for hedge fund managers (Strauss 2014). For some, a greater emphasis is placed on profits than on pupils.

Ramey also cites corruption and lack of transparency and accountability as problems facing elements of the school choice movement. Even more troubling are the strategies used to dissuade some students from applying in the first place, particularly "students with special needs, those with low test scores, English learners, or students in poverty" (Strauss 2014). Ramey observes that pop-up schools, in this case charter schools, exacerbate school segregation, take away resources from already under resourced schools, contribute to the closing of conventional public schools, and stifle creativity (Strauss 2014).

Furthermore, "smoke and mirrors" are essential to the promotion of pop-up schools. The over estimation of initial enrollment is an example (Castellanos 2012). Over estimating enrollment numbers is a strategy that may be used to sell the idea that a "new and improved" school is economically viable. The padding of anticipated enrollment data, can (and has) led to the transfer of seasoned teachers before the first progress reports are ever distributed to students and parents. "A consequence of this 'overstaffing' is the severing of the teacher-student relationship at one of its most critical moments. This may also result in the transfer of highly qualified teachers who are passionate about what they do, only to be replaced by inadequately trained teachers who lack the passion but possess requisite certifications to teach multiple subjects.

Deception is an important part of some of the strategies associated with contemporary educational reform. In addition to smoke and mirrors, pop-up schools often engage in a game akin to musical chairs. Teachers and principals are frequently moved around, or replaced with great frequency. Gone are those days when the schools were community-based with anchor teachers and anchor administrators. In pop-up schools, and in schools throughout the country, a new type of teacher has emerged due in large part of a perception that teachers are superfluous.

"Smoke and mirrors" and "musical chairs" are not the only misleading factors associated with pop-up schools and the larger educational reform movement. The use of the term *choice* is misleading. The use of the term *choice* to describe the alleged educational options available to students, teachers, administrators, and communities is not a coincidence.

Freedom to do something, or not to do something, is one of America's core values. Americans value the freedom of choice. It is at the heart of our representative democracy, albeit at times restrictive. The idea that parents should have the right to choose the schools their children will attend resonates with a lot of parents from across the racial, ethnic, and socioeconomic spectrum. We see parents exercising their freedom to choose all the time. Affluent parents often choose to purchase homes in neighborhoods with "good" public schools, or they may choose to pay for their child to attend a private school if designated public school is not up to their standards, however they choose to define the standards.

Less affluent parents may not have access to housing and rental markets where the "good" public schools are located and are therefore forced to send their children to designated school. It matters not whether the local school meets the standards of less affluent parents or not. Thus, the idea that less affluent parents might have the freedom to choose when it comes to where (and how) their children are educated seems like a blessing for economically and historically disadvantaged groups. It seems just. It seems like it is the American way. Finally, parents of color and less affluent families will have the same options as their white and more affluent counterparts. School choice programs, it is widely believed, level the playing field where education is concerned.

Words have power and the manner in which ideas are branded and marketed have meaning. Unfortunately, the mere use of the term "choice" does not mean that parents have either power or influence; rather, school choice provides an illusion of inclusion in a social system that-like all other social institutions in American society-is organized around the oppression and subordination of groups. It is not surprising then that racial differences exist and persist throughout the American public school system. It is also not hard to see how the deception in the contemporary educational reform movement appears to go relatively undetected by many, and actually gains the support of the very people who stand to be harmed the most.

In this so-called post-racial era, a period where it is alleged that race has declined in significance, school choice does the work of pre-*Brown v. Board of Topeka, Kansas* policies. One of the reasons this is occurring is due to what many American's see as a crisis in education, and some also see as an expected outcome of the institutionalization of inequality that bares the fruit of the seeds planted long ago. Consequently, persistent racial disparities in public education provide some of the best evidence of the oppressive and multilevel and multidimensional nature of the racialized social institution that is public education.

Unfortunately, far too many states and communities have adopted a big box model to fix the public school system in America, which has led to what I call the Wal-Martization of public education. Ott (2008) says the movement toward big box stores began in the early 1960s when the first Wal-Mart opened in response to "local consumer demand for the lower-cost, one-stop shopping format." Furthermore, Ott (2008) says the "so-called 'big-box' retail stores earned their names from their physical characteristics—their expansive size (typically 50,000 square feet or larger in the United States) and their customarily windowless, box-like appearance." Pop-up schools are increasing in response to demand from parents, students, employers, elected officials, and others for schools that are efficient, predicable, yield quantifiable results, and provide mechanisms for controlling students and teachers "by making tasks repetitive" and forcing teachers and students "not to think," in an effort "to maintain a tighter control over them" as outlined in Ritzer's (2007) theory of the McDonaldization of society.

In the big box model approach to educational reform, wealthy elites are motivated primarily by the pursuit of profits. Although wealthy elites may disagree on a host of social issues, they always agree that the pursuit of profit is more important than anything. Wealthy elites use their power and influence to control the labor market and the supply and demand for goods and services in ways that maximize profits. Given that maximizing profits is the ultimate goal, little if any consideration is given for how their actions impact non-elites. In the big box model competition from indigenous sources is eliminated. Eliminating competition and suppressing resistance efforts are necessary means toward the end goal of maximizing profits and are best suited in areas where access to social capital is relatively low, crime is relatively high, and labor and educational opportunities are few (Wolfe and Pyrooz 2014). Limited access to social capital means less resistance from the general public and high crime rates and lower labor and educational opportunities are often indicators of the socioeconomic status of the surrounding areas from which consumers are drawn. Thus, it is not surprising that pop-up schools are located in the same types of areas as big box stores, like Wal-Mart. It is also not surprising that the negative effects associated with the big box store model are also evidenced in this contemporary approach to reforming public education.

The main purpose of this book is to provide anyone with an interest in the future of public education, which should mean everyone, with the information required to elucidate the virtues of choosing the pathway that is today less traveled, and the perils of choosing the pathway paved with good and bad intensions.

Another purpose of this book is to describe and explain trends in public education in America and understand the roles of race and racism as race played an important role in maintaining and perpetuating a system of oppression whereby members of one group controlled the life chances and life opportunities of other groups. Restricting access to education was critical to maintaining the institution of slavery, to treating people of color as second class citizens thereafter, and to ensuring access to a large workforce equipped to do little else than fulfill the mundane, low paying, dead end jobs necessary to keep the wealth in the hands of the few and the misery in the hearts and minds of the masses.

In this book, I discuss changes in education over time. Loosely defined as variations on the general theme of educational reform, the educational trends discussed include the rise of charter schools, magnet schools, gifted and talent programs, the Common Core, standardized testing, dismissal of minority educators, and the closure of predominately black schools. These trends are placed within appropriate historical contexts. Although the aforementioned trends are receiving a lot of attention today, the origins of these trends date back to the mid-1600s when colonists began using the law to control the black population and lay the foundation for a racialized social system that exists today.

In this book I apply John Logan and Harvey Molotch's (2007) argument of the city as a growth machine; George Ritzer's (2007) argument of the McDonaldization of society; and economic critiques of Wal-Mart on the American economy (Wolfe and Pyrooz 2014) to explain the relationship between race, racism, and public education in America today. To facilitate the analysis of the connectedness of race, racism, and public education in America, I draw from critical race theory (Onwuachi-Willig 2009); Joe Feagin's (2010) white racial frame; and Eduardo Bonilla-Silva's (2013) color-blind racism. Drawing from the aforementioned perspectives, I examine public schools as profit machines and explain why majority minority schools are the ideal target.

I show how children of color, their parents, and their communities are part of an unethical educational experiment. This experiment happens to be unethical because of the failure to disclose the potential harm to subjects and the use of coercion and deception, which contribute to the absence of informed consent. The intended or unintended consequences of the contemporary educational reform movement, particularly as it relates to school choice, are to feed the school-to-prison pipeline; to use public schools to feed profit growth machine; and to develop real estate markets—not young minds.

Similar to other unethical experiments in the past, the human guinea pigs are people of color. With few exceptions, one is hard pressed to find the implementation of many educational reforms in school districts serving predominately white and/or relatively affluent communities. In instances where educational reforms impact predominately white and/or affluent communities the impact of such reforms is typically negligible, as such schools serve as the yardstick by which all other schools are evaluated. The use of predominately white and/or relatively affluent schools as the baseline for evaluating all other schools can best be described as educentrism.

Educentrism is similar to the concept ethnocentrism. Educentrism is the evaluation of public schools according to preconceptions originating in the standards and customs of predominately white and/or relatively affluent public and private schools. Educentrism has advantages and disadvantages associated with it. On the one hand, educentrism can create a collective acknowledgement of the critical role public education plays in our society. At the heart of the myth of meritocracy is the belief that through hard work and determination anyone can achieve the American Dream. Education is often conceptualized as the key that opens the door to success in America. The idealistic view of education also holds that our public education system must prepare students for the labor force, for post-secondary studies, and for life-long learning.

On the other hand, educentrism can also create a feeling of supremacy over schools where the students, teachers, administrators, parents, and communities are viewed as inherently inferior and not as disadvantaged based upon limited by access to valued resources. Educentrism can also serve to provide a justification for victim blaming and a rationalization for racial, gender, and class ideologies. Given that public schools that are hailed as the standard by which all other schools are judged are often majority white and/or majority affluent, individuals, neighborhoods and districts that are deviate from the standard are often viewed as innately inferior and culturally deviant.

Educentrism means that society imposes a set of standards and benchmarks on public schools everywhere knowing full well that selected schools will not meet such standards and that the purported failure of said schools means differentiated access to wealth, status, and power in our society will remain and will continue to be differentiated by many social characteristics, especially race.

The role of race in decisions about educational policies cannot be overstated. Race is treated in contemporary times much like a computer hacker or computer virus. It is out there—somewhere—but no one worries much about it, or even acknowledges the potential threat, until it is too late and entire networks or individual workstations are infected. Far too many people claim not to see race and until they are forced to at least consider it. The images of the lifeless bodies of unarmed black men lying in public areas are some of the instances that can cause racial optimists to pause, if only for a moment. The images of young people of color attending under resourced schools, dropping out of school, bused hours away from home to segregated schools, and the school-to-prison pipeline, should also awaken in us a sense of urgency, a feeling of righteous indignation.

Big Box Schools: Race, Education, and the Danger of the Wal-Martization of Public Schools in America includes case studies, which highlight how students, parents, teachers, and community leaders are working to change the trajectory of public education in America and improve educational outcomes for all students, but especially for black students. The case studies even include some programs born out of the school choice movement that are uncharacteristically neighborhood-based, such as a magnet school in Buffalo, New York.

The target audiences for this book are graduate students, scholars, and professions. Graduate students in education, sociology, political science, urban studies, community studies, and African American Studies will find the book most useful. Educators, education advocates, and education policymakers will also find the book both useful and informative.

The book begins with the history of race and public education in America. Chapter 2 highlights the efforts to limit the ability of people of color to learn to read and write by the dominant racial group. The issues regarding access to a good quality education after the historic *Brown v Board of Education of Topka* case has been explored. I debunk the myth that blacks, the poor, and renters are disinvested in public education, lack civic engagement, and therefore have little interest in what happens to public education. I argue that many in the aforementioned groups are hyper invested in public education and civically engaged. However, the poor, blacks, and renters are often deliberately misinformed about their rights and agency where public education is concerned.

Chapter 3 deals with an in-depth look of the American public educational system as a machine of profit maximization. Much like urban growth machines, educational profit machines are fueled by insatiable desire to see a return on an investment not into the people affected by the decisions made; rather, an investment into an enterprise where academic success is important only to the extent that it yields more profit.

Chapter 4 talks about the main features of the Wal-Mart model and the ways in which the model is used in public schools across the country, but especially in predominately minority communities. On the same note, chapter 5 includes an in-depth analysis of implications of what I call the Wal-Martization of American public education; namely, the impact on education and today's black working-class.

Chapter 6 consists of a thorough discussion about race, education, and plutocrats in America. In chapter 7 the displacement of indigenous organizations and educational leaders by non-educators with the resources to exert their will on the masses has been explored. Chapter 8 shows how some communities across the country are fighting back and changing the trajectory of public education in America. I also introduce an index to determine the extent to which educational reform efforts place communities at risk for harm. The concluding chapter includes strategies for improving the American public educational system.

Chapter Two

History of Race and Public Education in America

Individuals who share similar physical characteristics are members of the same racial group. However, sharing similar physical characteristics is not what is most significant about how and why our society—in historical and in contemporary times—groups people. What is most significant about the classification of people by race are the social meanings, public policies, and private practices that we attach to each category. When we elevate the significance of membership in one group, we lower the significance of membership in another group. When we create public polices to benefit one racial group, we exclude other groups from such privileges. When we show deference to one group, we often show distain for other groups.

Race and racism—the multilevel and multidimensional system of oppression where a dominant group scapegoats and oppresses one or more subordinate group—are important predictors of virtually all sociological outcomes. Race and racism are central, foundational features of our American social structure and as such, permeate every social institution, including education. Depending upon your perspective, race and racism either explain the existence and persistence of disparities in education, or race and racism are convenient excuses used by people of color to mask their individual shortcomings and inheritable and transferable cultural deficiencies.

In this chapter I examine the history of race in America and the role of race and racism in the formation, reformation, and transformation of the American public school system over time. I examine the ways in which race and racism were used as tools to suppress and oppress people of color, and at the same time used by people of color to fight back against a system set-up to ensure their failure. I begin in antebellum America where laws were on the books prohibiting the enslaved from learning to read and write. I discuss the growth of free black communities and the growth of free black schools. I examine variations within the black community as to the purpose of education in the lives of those ushering in the twentieth century. I discuss the challenges facing black students, parents, and educators before and after *Brown.*

RACE, EDUCATION, AND ANTEBELLUM AMERICA

Race is a social construct. The concept of race is one that was created by human beings. What it means to have membership in a given racial group varies across place and time. For much of America's history being black meant living at the bottom rung of society without just cause. Hines et. al (2011) notes that by 1619 there were over thirty people of African ancestry in the Chesapeake area. This group undoubtedly understood what it meant to be a stranger in a strange land. Hines et. al (2011) describes the group, not as slaves, but as unfree for the following reasons, "First, unlike the Portuguese and the Spanish, the English had no law for slavery. Second, at least those Angolans who bore such names as Pedro, Isabella, Antoney, and Angelo were Christians, and—according to English custom and morality in 1619— Christians could not be enslaved" (p. 63). Over time whites in the Chesapeake area began to draw a clear line between themselves and people of African ancestry and used the law and violence as forms of social control.

Racial ideology, a web of ideas based upon the supremacy of one racial group and the inferiority of all others, played an important role in the establishment of black servitude in America. The dehumanization of people of African ancestry was necessary to facilitate the transition from an economy that was highly reliant upon white indentured servants to one that was almost totally dependent on the unpaid labor of chattel slavery. Fewer Europeans were feeling pushed out of their homelands due to a lack of economic opportunities, which created a labor shortage at a time when Britain's role and influence in the Atlantic slave trade grew and the costs of African slaves decreased.

Overtime the restrictions placed upon every aspect of black life was tightened. By the 1640s, blacks did not have the right to bear arms and could no longer become Christians and for the first time on record, a man of African descent was sentenced to servitude for life. John Punch was an indentured servant who fled with several white indentured servants before the end of their service. All were punished when they were apprehended, but only John Punch, the lone African in the group, was sentenced to serve forever.

Laws defining the condition of a child born to an enslaved woman appeared in the House of Burgesses in the early 1660s. The rules that applied to the enslaved routinely violated what was common practice under British law.

Under chattel slavery, the status of the child followed that of the mother. "The change permitted masters to exploit their black female servants sexually without having to acknowledge the children who might result from such contacts" (Hines et. al 2011, p. 65). Slave codes also played important roles in constructing a racialized social structure, which led to the unequal treatment of blacks in every corner of society. Several slave codes applied specifically to education.

An act in South Carolina assessed a fine of one hundred pounds to anyone assisting a person of color with learning to read or write, or employing a person of color in an occupation involving reading and writing. The act from the 1700s reads,

> Whereas, the having slaves taught to write, or suffering them to be employed in writing, may be attended with great inconveniences; Be it enacted, that all and every person and persons whatsoever, who shall hereafter teach or cause any slave or slaves to be taught to write, or shall use or employ any slave as a scribe, in any manner of writing whatsoever, hereafter taught to write, every such person or persons shall, for every such offense, forfeit the sum of one hundred pounds, current money. (http://www.pbs.org/wnet/slavery/experience/education/docs1.html)

South Carolina was not the only area to view the education of the enslaved as a threat to the status quo. A 1819 Virginia code made it unlawful for blacks, regardless of their status as free, enslaved, black, or mulatto, from assembling in schools for the purpose of teaching reading and writing—day or night. The code also granted the right of officers to "to inflict corporal punishment on the offender or offenders, at the discretion of any justice of the peace, not exceeding twenty lashes."

Similar prohibitions involving the education of free and enslaved blacks existed throughout the land. According to Gilder Lehrman Center for the Study of Slavery, Resistance, and Abolition at Yale University, whites in Georgia could be fined $500 and face imprisonment for teaching a person of African ancestry to read or write. If a black person taught another person of color to read or write, even if that person was their very own child, he was to be whipped or fined at the discretion of the court, according to the 1829 law. Louisiana lawmakers decided on fewer options for violators of the state's ban on the education of free or enslaved blacks. One year in prison was the penalty in Louisiana.

Nevertheless, many blacks possessed a strong desire to learn to read and write and many were aided by the establishment of schools in free black communities and even in schools created by the army during the Civil War, according to historian Eric Foner. It is therefore not surprising that efforts to dismantle the institution of slavery were buttressed by an increase in the number of free blacks and the number of literate blacks.

The ability to read and write was a powerful tool for abolitionists as evidenced in the eloquent writings and speeches by people like Frederick Douglass and so many others, many whose names we may never know. Learning to read and write was a top priority for freed men and women after the institution of slavery officially ended with the adoption of the Thirteenth Amendment. Establishing schools was right up there with reuniting family members and acquiring land. Love, land, and literacy were the primary areas of concern for blacks during the period known as Reconstruction.

RACE, EDUCATION, AND THE RECONSTRUCTION ERA

After centuries of living under a system where every aspect of black life was controlled by the white power structure, blacks finally arrived at a time in their collective history where many thought they would control their own destinies. Not only did slavery end, but also constitutional rights were extended to blacks, and black men everywhere had the right to vote. Blacks could vote during Reconstruction in places where they could not even walk years earlier. Blacks were elected to offices at various levels of government. Blacks established independent churches, mutual aid societies, and even schools. The Freedman's Bureau was established to assist blacks in making the transition from slavery to freedom; it too established schools for freedmen, women, and children.

Living under the oppressive system of slavery taught people of color a lot, including how central becoming educated was to attaining political power and influence. Clarence Walker summarizes the significance of education to the newly freed population beautifully in the following statement, "For many black people in the South, to learn how to read and write to figure and how to somehow move in a world of letters, was a revolutionary act, because it now gave them the skills and the tools whereby they could combat the racism that had oppressed them for centuries" (http://www.pbs.org/wgbh/amex/reconstruction/schools/sf_postwar.html).

In 1870 the Preparatory High School for Colored Youth was organized in Washington, DC. Allison Stewart writes about the historic school in her book, *First Class: The Legacy of Dunbar, America's First Black Public High School*. Stewart documents the role of Ms. Myrtilla Miner. Ms. Miner was the visionary behind the school. It was her goal to train a generation of teachers. With the financial support of famed author Harriet Beecher Stowe's brother, William Beecher, Miner was able to acquire a building for her and her pupils. Mary Jane Patterson led the school. Ms. Patterson required students to demonstrate proficiency in the areas of physics, geometry and geography. The school was renamed in 1916 to honor poet, Paul Laurence Dunbar. Graduates from the first black public high school included a U.S. Army general and a U.S. Cabinet member in the Johnson administration, to name a few.

Black schools were organized in places such as Louisa County, Virginia. The county was created in 1742, according to records kept by the Louisa County Historical Society. At the time the county was established there were no formal efforts to limit access to education for either free or enslaved blacks. Concerns that blacks might join forces and rebel against the system that regarded them as less than human beings led to the passage of Black Laws in Virginia in 1831, including a law that banned teaching blacks to read or write.

Like many places throughout the South that relied on the unpaid labor of generations of black men, women, and children for everything from the rearing of their children to an area's tax base, struggled after the end of the Civil War. "Combined tax revenues in 1870 were one-fourth of what they had been in 1863, when taxes on slaves alone earned the county $58,389."

Virginia, and other places throughout the region, created constitutions following the Civil War and the 1869 Virginia document allowed for free public education for blacks and whites. Although blacks and whites could have access to a free public education, blacks and whites could not attend schools together.

Not only did blacks and whites attend separate schools, the schools were by no measure equal. Black schools were often "poorly equipped log cabins, church buildings or rooms in private homes." The first public school for black children opened in 1883 at the county courthouse. All teachers were paid with county funds and were paid the same, regardless of race or gender. However, "Larger political and social movements began throughout the South that would reverse progress toward equal citizenship for free blacks achieved during Reconstruction." Many southern states constructed and ratified new constitutions, which included efforts to disenfranchise black voters through the use of poll taxes and literacy tests.

Kentucky was also home to a number of notable black schools during Reconstruction. The schools for blacks in Henderson County, Kentucky received support from the Freedmen's Bureau. According to research conducted by scholars at the University of Kentucky, black schools "didn't last: the teachers were threatened and run out of town." The researchers also note there was a black school in Cairo during the 1870s. Dr. Pickney Thompson wrote an act in 1871, which led to the creation of the school. Thompson and all of the trustees for the school were white. The school superintendent, Samuel Harris was also white. Harris was also a teacher at the school. Several black female educators also worked with Harris at different times throughout the first part of the school's ninety-year history. The school housed nearly 150 students. The school rapidly grew in terms of the building and in terms of enrollment. By 1880 there were sixteen schools for blacks in the county. Over 600 students were enrolled in Henderson County blacks schools.

One of the most significant Supreme Court cases in the nation's history was decided in the latter part of the nineteenth century and had a tremendous impact on race and education in America for the generations that followed. The case involving Homer Plessy was meant to challenge a system of racial oppression supported by public policies and private practices. Plessy, who could pass for white, intentionally rode in the white section of a train in New Orleans, Louisiana. Plessy was arrested and, as planned, challenged the law. Plessy made the argument that the separation of the races on trains was in direct violation of the Fourteenth Amendment, marking blacks as inferior to whites. The case made it to the U.S. Supreme Court where the justices decided, in a vote of seven to one, that the law was not in violation of Plessy's constitutional rights because the Fourteenth Amendment was to bring about equality between the races, "but in the nature of things it could not have been intended to abolish distinctions based upon color, or to endorse social, as distinguished from political, equality . . . If one race be inferior to the other socially, the Constitution of the United States cannot put them upon the same plane" (http://www.uscourts.gov/educational-resources/get-involved/federal-court-activities/brown-board-education-re-enactment/history.aspx)."The Court approved the principle of separate but equal, which for the next half-century and more was used to justify laws mandating segregation in every area of life in the South, from transportation to education" (Thompson n. d.)

Harlan, the only justice to vote in Plessy's favor, made two critical points in what Charles Thompson of the University of Louisville, Louis D. Brandeis School of Law calls "Harlan's Great Dissent." Harlan, a native of Kentucky, argued,

> In the eyes of the law, there is in this country no superior, dominant, ruling class of citizens. There is no caste here. Our constitution is colorblind, and neither knows nor tolerates classes among citizens. In respect of civil rights, all citizens are equal before the law. The humblest is the peer of the most powerful. . . . The arbitrary separation of citizens on the basis of race, while they are on a public highway, is a badge of servitude whole inconsistent with the civil freedom and the equality before the law established by the Constitution. It cannot be justified upon any legal grounds.

Harlan's words revealed just how wide the gap was between ideal and real culture in the late nineteenth century. While justice was supposed to be blind, there were countless examples of unequal treatment under the law based solely upon one's race. There was indeed a caste system in America and it was race-based. The constitution was race-specific in its historic inclusion of some groups, and the exclusion of others. Not only were social divisions among citizen tolerated, but also the existence of such divisions and the privileges afforded selected classes had the full faith and confidence of the government at all levels. Harlan was correct in stating the separation of citizens was both arbitrary and race-based. There were no clear distinct races, but there was a racial classification system in place that was hierarchical in nature. Skin color served as the most visible "badge of servitude" and was at once inconsistent with what American claimed to value, but wholly consistent with the manner in which blacks were historically treated in the United States.

Harlan also stated, "What can more certainly arouse race hate, what more certainly can create and perpetuate a feeling of distrust between the races, than state enactments, which, in fact, proceed on the ground that colored citizens are so inferior and degraded that they cannot be allowed to site in public coaches occupied by white citizens? That, as all will admit, is the real meaning of such legislation."

Harlan rightly notes that the sin is not only in the mistreatment of people of color, but that the chief perpetrator is the government, which should act to protect the rights of citizens, not restrict them and give cover to those that would infringe upon the rights of other Americans. Laws separating the races serve as a constant reminder of the unjustifiable subordinate position of people of color in American society.

Justice Harlan's words were all the more remarkable when one recalls his background as a former slave owner who once declared the Emancipation Proclamation unconstitutional. Several years after the Thirteenth Amendment outlawed slavery, Harlan declared slavery as one of the worse things that ever occurred in America and expressed gratitude the institution was no more. Some contend Harlan's epiphany about the institution of slavery had more to do with his political aspirations than his genuine belief in the equality of the races. Others say his close relationship with his half-brother who was a slave played an important role. Whatever the reason, Harlan's words would motivate Thurgood Marshall and others to bring about a legal end to the separate by equal doctrine (Thompson n. d., http://www.law.louisville.edu/library/collections/harlan/dissent).

RACE, EDUCATION, AND A NEW CENTURY

The period between the end of Reconstruction and eve of the Great Depression was an important time in our nation's history, especially where race and education were concerned. Between the 1880s and the early 1920s the United States experienced a great population shift. Millions of people from Southern, Eastern, and Central Europe immigrated to the United States and Americans struggled to identify how these strangers from a distant shore might one day become Americans. People of color undoubtedly wondered what the presence of these immigrants would mean for their employment outlook and continued struggle to be treated as full citizens. Stanley Lieberson described how public education system was used to Americanize millions of men, women, and children who were initially treated as separate and inferior races when compared to people of European ancestry who were already in the United States.

The new immigrants differed from the old immigrants in important ways. Old immigrants in 1910 were literate and many new immigrants were illiterate. For example, according to Liberson's book, *A Piece of the Pie,* less than 1 percent of Scandinavian, Scottish, Welsh, and English immigrants were illiterate in 1910 compared to over half of immigrants from southern Italy. Nearly 40 percent of Russian immigrants were illiterate in 1910. By 1917 a literacy test was introduced to limit immigration from Southern, Eastern, and Central Europe. Restrictive immigration laws followed which curtailed immigration from selected areas in the years that followed and the laws remained in place until the mid-1960s.

Liberson (1980) described the function of schools in great detail. "The schools serve not only a cultural function, such as preserving and transmitting the past, but also they prepare people for jobs, social class, and social mobility (p. 124). Liberson (1980) also addressed the differences between the approaches to education for blacks and whites immigrations between the late 1880s and the early 1900s. New immigrants were concentrated in urban areas in the North, while most blacks were still living in the South in the large numbers. Schools in the North existed to assimilate white immigrants, "teaching the English language, develop loyalty to the new nation through an understanding of its history and opportunities, create the habits of dress, cleanliness, and demeanor that were desired, and generate a literate population that could vote wisely and also contribute positively to the labor force" (Liberson 1980, p. 135). On the other hand, the function of schools for blacks in the South was to prepare blacks for life at the bottom of the economic and social structure. Compulsory school attention was connected to the different approaches to education for blacks and whites.

Not only were the approaches to education different for new immigrants and for blacks, but access to resources varied. Data from 1930 reveal racial disparities school expenditures in Southern states. For every dollar spent on white schools in Mississippi only 21 cents was spent on black schools during the same year. In Louisiana the black-white ratio was .33 and .79 in Oklahoma. Teacher salaries were substantially lower for teachers in white schools than teachers in black schools. In counties where the black students made up at least half of the school-aged population teachers in black schools earned about a tenth of what teachers in white schools earned for the 1930–1931 school year. The disparities were not as great in counties where the black population was smaller. In counties where black students represented between 0 and 12.4 percent of the school-aged population, teachers in black schools earned about $9.00, while teachers in white schools earned about $14.00.

Racial disparities in education where continuously challenged, but a notable shift occurred in the first half of the twentieth century. There was a notable shift from the creation of same-race schools towards the desegregation of schools. The movement was part of a larger effort to integrate American society, not because being in close proximity to whites was the goal, but because whites had access to resources and to the rights and privileges that should have been made available to all. Efforts to desegregate schools occurred in the North and in the South. A number of legal efforts standout, including the case involving Donald Gaines Murray in the 1930s, the Brook School case in the 1940s, and Brown and Brown II in the 1950s.

Murray was born in Philadelphia, Pennsylvania and applied to the University of Maryland School of law on January 24, 1935. Murray's application was rejected because he was black. Murray appealed to the Board of Regents of the University of Maryland School but his bid was unsuccessful. Murray was aided by a number of lawyers in his desire to take legal action against the University of Maryland and Thurgood Marshall and Charles Hamilton Houston eventually presented his case. Murray's suit was based upon the fact that the State of Maryland did not provide a law school for blacks and that the university's policy of racial segregation was unconstitutional. The president of the university was ultimately ordered to admit Donald Gaines Murray to the University of Maryland School of Law where he eventually graduated in 1938. The opinion stated that the State of Maryland assumed the function of education in the law, "but has omitted students of one race from the only adequate provision made for it, and omitted them solely because of color. If those students are to be offered equal treatment in the performance of the function, they must, at present, be admitted to the one school provided." The case played a significant role in the breaking down of barriers to education throughout the State of Maryland and helped Thurgood Marshall prepare for future cases, such as the cases in the Brook School in Hillburn, New York.

In the late 1930s, schools in the State of New York were ordered to integrate. However, schools in the town of Hillburn, located in Rockland County, New York, remained separate and unequal. Brook School was the only school in the county, and one of three in upstate New York, with black teachers. The school was built in 1889 to educate black children and was in such poor condition that parents described it as "a veritable fire trap, with inadequate exit facilities" (Nordstrom 2005, p. 165). In fact, a report from the U.S. Office of Education called for the closure of the school. There was another school in Hillburn, which was attended by white children. The Main School had eight rooms and was for whites only. By September 1943, the black parents mobilized to force the integration of schools in Hillburn. Black parents refused to send their children to Brook School and with the support of the National Association for the Advancement of Colored People (NAACP) appealed to the New York State Commissioner of Education. Thurgood Marshall argued the case on behalf of the parents and the civil rights organization. The First Lady of the theater, Helen Hayes, also played a role in bringing the case to the NAACP's attention. According to Rollins and Hines (1995) book *All is Never Said: The Narrative of Odette Harper Hines*, Hayes employed several light-skinned blacks and was disturbed to find children in Hillburn were attending schools segregated by race. Hayes and a committee from the newly formed Hillburn NAACP visited the NAACP office before deciding to strike.

Commissioner, Dr. George Stoddard, contacted the county superintendent and expressed the need to end segregation in the school district. The district drew new boundary lines for the two schools, which resulted in the inclusion of about one-third of the students at the former Brook School. No whites would attend the Brook School. Parents at Brook School kept up the pressure, even subjected themselves to fines for keeping their children from school. A site visit was eventually conducted and Commissioner Stoddard ordered Brook School closed. All the children and teachers were transferred to the Main School. White parents withdrew their children from the Main School in response to the closure of Brook School. Thurgood Marshall's first school desegregation victory occurred outside the Deep South, but he is most closely associated with the landmark *Brown v. Board of Education, Topeka, Kansas*.

BROWN V. BOARD OF EDUCATION: A LANDMARK LEGACY

Oliver Brown was the first of five plaintiffs, hence the name of the historic case. He brought the case against the school board for its refusal to allow his daughter, Linda, to attend the all-white school in their neighborhood. At the time of Brown's suit, the Board of Education in Topeka, Kansas operated four black schools and almost 20 white schools. The *Brown* case would bring a legal end to the separate but equal doctrine established in the *Plessy v. Ferguson* case.

While the *Brown* case is remembered fondly as a landmark decision and one of the greatest achievements of the modern day civil rights movement, the legacy of the 1954 Supreme decision has been called into question. Derrick Bell declared the *Brown* decision "dead and beyond resuscitation" in a publication that appeared in the *New York Law School Law Review*. Bell explored why *Brown* is remembered and why the case achieved landmark status. Bell said it was not until 1970 that the courts actually began enforcing school desegregation in meaningful ways. He admitted that he did not agree with legal scholars who warned *Brown* would have devastating effects on the education of black and white children in America because he was so committed to the philosophy of integration as the most effective way to address the inferior education afforded to black children throughout the U.S., but particularly in the South.

Bell conceded in the 2005 article that *Brown* was irrelevant. The case was symptomatic of a larger trend, but ongoing narrative. The law was used to maintain the racial status quo. In other words, "civil rights law approximates the jurisprudence of the era following Reconstruction when *Plessy v. Ferguson* was decided. Bell also argued that courts assume that race no longer matters under the "guise of colorblindness" (Bell 2005, p. 1055). One consequence was that courts viewed race-specific efforts to address racial inequality on the same level as acts created to maintain a ranking system based on race. Thus, affirmative action was characterized as a form of reverse discrimination.

There were at least four important takeaways from *Brown* decision, according to Bell (2005). First, the school desegregation case was the latest in a long list of examples of policymakers addressing racial justice issues only when it was politically and economically expedient and beneficial for the interest of the policymakers. Second, a convergence of black and white interest was more important to gaining relief from racial injustice than the extent and duration of the harm suffered. The third lesson was that the remedy for addressing the racial injustice will be abandoned when the remedy is perceived as a threat to the privileged status of whites, especially whites in the middle- and upper-classes. Finally, Bell (2005) said we learned the *Brown* decision was a disaster for black children. Black children in desegregated schools were disciplined more often than their white counterparts. Black children in desegregated schools were also taught by individuals and in environments with a lack of cultural interest and were often placed in tracks that did not prepare them for academic success.

Bizer and Ellis (2006) studied the impact of *Brown* where it all started in Topkea, Kansas more than a half century later. Using a normative theoretical approach, which says prejudice and discrimination are influenced by societal norms and are found in situations that serve to promote tolerance or intolerance of minority groups, Bizer and Ellis (2006) concluded *Brown* was slow to change or influence discrimination.

Dr. Kwando Kinshasa (2006) wrote about the impact of *Brown* not only on education, but also on the larger social justice movement. The influence of *Brown* on the Montgomery Bus Boycott was one example of how the approach to addressing school segregation set the agenda for fighting social justice issues for decades to come and the effects of the approach are still felt today. Kinshasa (2006) said the Montgomery Bus Boycott was the first test of the *Brown* case. Both challenged "white Americans desire to maintain economic hegemony as well as political and psychological control of society through racial segregation (p.17). The focus for both was on social integration without adequate consideration for economic parity. Bell (2005) would agree with Kinshasa (2006) as evidenced in his argument that civil rights activists focused more on the separate part of the historic doctrine and not enough on the equal. Bell (2005) said if the emphasis was on the equal, black children would be better off. Kinshasa (2006) said, African American community development would be leaps and bounds ahead of where it is in contemporary America were integration and economic empowerment given top billing.

Dancy and Brown (2008) observed that the continued focus on integration was apparent not only in elementary and secondary schools, but it was also evident in colleges and universities throughout the country. The focus on many colleges-both at Historically Black Colleges and Universities (HBCUs) and Predominately White Institutions (PWIs)-was to change the racial demographics of the student and staff. The researchers say the *Fordice* case was responsible for shifting emphasis from fiscal and academic equity to "redesignation and racial recomposition of student populations." This race transdemography was often manifested in the recruitment of whites at HBCUs and blacks at PWIs, and could best be understood as an unintended consequence of the *Brown* decision.

Data on the continued segregation of black and white children in schools provides some of the best evidence of the unfilled promise of the *Brown* decision. Reardon and Owens (2014) report on the trends and consequences of school segregation in a recent article in the *Annual Review of Sociology.* The researchers focus on two eras, 1954–1980 and 1980 and beyond. During the first period understudy Reardon and Owens (2014) found that black-white segregation declined substantially, especially in the South, but not until after 1968 when freedom of choice desegregation plans declined. Under freedom of choice plans, it was the responsibility of black families to enroll their children in white schools, regardless of the racial antagonism that persisted in many areas where residents remained resistant to the idea of integration. Consequently, more than three-fourths of black students still attended segregated schools.

Green v. County School Board of New Kent County forced school districts to create and implement more meaningful desegregation strategies. Within a decade, school districts across the country were under court-ordered plans to desegregate. By 1980, about 30 percent of black students attended schools were 90 percent or more of students were black. Reardon and Owens (2014) found a lack of consensus as to how best to characterize the period following the 1980s. Some researchers characterized the period, "by a gradual trend of resegregation of black students" (p. 203), while "other scholars have argued that segregation has not risen significantly in the last two decades" (p. 203).

The debate about the trajectory of school segregation was contingent upon the measure of segregation used. Reardon and Owens (2014) conclude, "It seems fair to say that the last 25 years have been characterized by largely stable patterns of sorting students among schools (unevenness), whereas the racial/ethnic composition of the student population has changed substantially, a pair of trends that yields declining black-white exposure measures but no significant change in unevenness measures of segregation. Whether this represents resegregation or stagnation depends upon one's theory of how and why segregation matters" (p. 204).

John Logan's report on school segregation titled, "Whose Schools are Failing?" contended that much of the attention on the segregation of school has focused on the extent to which children go to schools with children from different backgrounds and not enough attention is devoted to the quality of the schools all students attend. "Researchers emphasize that segregation undermines equal opportunity not only because it separates children by race but because it leaves minority children in inferior schools" (Logan 2010, p. 1). The children most frequently left behind in failing schools are children of color, says Logan. "The assumption is that, all else equal, it is advantageous to attend a school where more students are successful. This is why No Child Left Behind Act (NCLB), signed into law in 2002, introduced mechanisms to identify failing schools" (Logan 2010, p. 1).

NCLB was arguably one of the most controversial educational policies implemented in recent years. NCLB represented a shift in the role of the federal government in public education. Kraft and Furlong (2013) provide a brief overview of education policy in the United States and the changing role of the federal government. According to Kraft and Furlong (2013), founding fathers saw education as inextricably linked to the ideal of democracy. For Thomas Jefferson education provided "an avenue to ensure the continuation of U.S. democracy. How can people be active, engaged participants in democratic processes if they lack the ability to read and understand the issues? Second, education helps to assimilate large numbers of immigrants. Finally, it is the primary mechanism for social mobility in the United States, as the educated are better able to secure jobs that raise their economic and social status" (Kraft and Furlong, 2013 p. 365).

Kraft and Furlong (2013) added the justification for government involvement in education was both moral and political. Government support education would help communicate the nation's goals and values among its citizenry and help prospective candidates win public office. "Traditionally, public education has been in the hands of state and local government" (Kraft and Furlong 2013, p. 365). State governments have long been in the practice of establishing curriculum, training educators, and funding schools. The bulk of educational policy is historically sharped at the local level. Kraft and Furlong (2013) were careful to note that the role local actors shaping educational policy does not mean that the federal government has had no role in shaping educational policy. The role of the federal government in shaping educational policy has grown over times, especially since the mid-1960s.

The Elementary and Secondary Education Act (ESEA) was the first major education legislation Congress passed, according to Kraft and Furlong (2013). The law increased federal support for education for primary and secondary schools. ESEA "signaled the beginning of increased federal interest in public education" (Kraft and Furlong 2013, p. 366). The increased interest in public education has "raised not only suspicion on the part of policymakers who oppose it but also questions about equity and freedom" (Kraft and Furlong 2013, p. 367).

Kraft and Furlong (2013) outlined a host of issues facing education, many of which increased or emerged after the federal government began take a more active role and interest in public education, especially primary and secondary education. These problems including "funding for public schools, the separation of church and state, the quality of education, school vouchers, and the merit of a host of proposals—such as teacher standards and testing requirements—for improving the performance of public schools" (Kraft and Furlong 2013, p. 368).

Funding of public schools using local property taxes presents a set of problems because property taxes do not keep up with the price of inflation and the revenue generated from local property taxes various greatly. Some states have taken to alternative measures for generating revenues for education, including the use of sales tax in places like Michigan. School funding is a significant issue because it impacts the quality of education provided and received.

The separation of church and state is an issue related to education, not only with respect to prayer and schools and whether or not creationism should be taught, but with respect to the public funding of religious schools. Defining and measuring the quality of education is yet another issue facing public education that the federal government has decided to weigh-in on in ways it had not previously. Some areas of concern include the quality of instruction and instructors and teaching tenure, concerns reflected in more testing requirements for students that are tied to the evaluation of not only students, but the evaluation of teachers, schools, and districts.

President Bush issued NCLB after his first legislative proposal following a close election against Vice President Al Gore. What began as a relatively short concept paper soon became a bill that was over one thousand pages in length. Standards and assessments were a key part of the legislation as were provisions for accountability at the state and district levels. An issue that was traditionally associated with the Democratic Party in America was gaining steam among conservatives and Republicans across the nation. The bill would include measures for assessing the process of elementary and secondary schools through the nation and would assign sanctions to schools that failed to make the grade. "The formula had three elements: (1) By the year 2014, all students must be performing in reading, mathematics, and science at the 'proficient' level; (2) in each school each year, student 'adequate yearly progress' must increase at such a rate that 100 percent proficiency would be met by 2014; and (3) the annual rate of progress applies not only to the aggregate student enrollment of a school, district, or state but also to 'disaggregated' groups of students according to income, race, gender, English language ability, and special education status. If any of the groups are below expected progress rates, the entire school is considered 'failing' and in need of improvement to be realized through presidential sanctions" (New York State Education Department 2006, p. 74).

Schools not meeting state standards for two years in a row would receive the designation of "needing improvement." Schools in need of improvement would need to develop a two-year plan to demonstrate how the school will reverse course. Students in schools in need of improvement could transfer to another public school that was not in need of improvement. Students could transfer to public charter schools, for example. In some cases, the only schools not in need of improvement in a district might be a public charter school.

If the school still does not meet the state standard for a third consecutive year, the school must still offer students the option of transferring to another public school. Also, students from low-income backgrounds would have access to supplemental services, such as tutoring. Schools failing a fourth year require corrective action by the district. Corrective action might include the removal of staff or even the introduction of a new curriculum. Again, school choice and supplemental services would still be options. Districts must restructure schools that fail to meet state-identified standards after a fifth year. Restructuring a school "may include reopening the school as a charter school, replacing all or most of the school staff, or turning over school operations either to the state or to a private company with a demonstrated record of effectiveness" (New York State Department of Education 2006, p. 74–5).

The aforementioned sanctions along with the requirement that schools and districts test every student in grades three through eight in reading, math and science on an annual basis were among the most controversial components of NCLB. Why did Repu'licans suddenly embrace a political issue that has been a cornerstone of the Democratic Party for many years? According to a report from the New York State Department of Education, the president convinced key members of his party that Republicans needed to take a leading role in preparation for the important midterm elections. "The emphasis on accountability overrode the conservatives' dislike of federal intervention and more spending" (p. 75). Many Democrats eventually jumped on board because some components of the bill included concepts from legislation pushed through by democrats previously. Other Democrats joined because the president threatened to cut education funds. Many Democrats also feared some in their party would join the reform movement and pass a package that would allow for vouchers for private school students (New York State Department of Education 2006). In the end, the soul of public education was sold for political gain. Both parties were devastated by a close election, the outcome of which was decided in the courts, and immediately began jockeying for position to avoid another close contest in future elections. Public education is so closely tied to issues of race, gender, class, and so forth, that it was an ideal place to play politically. Calling for reform in public education was an acknowledgement that the educational system was not serving all students. Including language in NCLB, which appeared to reflect a form of compassionate conservatism toward historically disadvantaged groups, drew many loyal Democratic policymakers, community leaders, and parents, toward support for the bill, until folks began reading the fine print and really began to understand the immediate and long-term effects to the legislation.

National School Boards Association, the American Association of School Administrators, the National Education Association, and the National Conference of State Legislators were among the early groups to voice opposition to NCLB. The groups essentially argued that NCLB was an unfunded mandate. Schools, districts, and states where being told to do something, but not given the resources to make it happen. This is not a new problem of course. Throughout our history there are examples where laws have been passed aimed at addressing and redressing inequalities but without the appropriate funding levels, or even human resources required to effectively carry out the spirit of the law, causing many to question whether or not the intent all along was to increase the political capital of the party promoting the legislation, or to quell a rebellious spirit among a group of oppressed people. Lack of adequate funding from the Freedmen's Bureau to NCLB is part of our American legacy on race.

Critics of NCLB expressed concerns about the involvement of corporations. The Summer 2002 issue of *Policy Report* outlined the major concerns. The involvement of the business community in educational reform creates pipelines from schools to workplace skills; ties funding from the federal government to outcomes; decreases regulatory and development role of federal government in education; and places the day-to-day operations of schools in the hands of the business community and out of the hands of educators. While there is certainly a place for public-private partnerships in education, the involvement of the business community in educational reform in recent years may best be understood as one that mistakenly equates education with workforce development.

Diane Ravitch, a former Assistant Secretary of Education in the President George W. Bush administration, is now a well-known critic of NCLB. In her book *The Death and Life of the Great American School System,* she addresses a host of issues, and places great emphasis on standardized testing. "Incentives and sanctions were not the right levels to improve education; incentives and sanctions may be right for business organizations, where the bottom line—profit—is the highest priority, but they are not right for schools" (Ravitch 2010). Public education has increasingly become more about profit than about the exchange of knowledge. Profit is the end goal for individuals and corporations behind quasi-public schools. Profit is the end goal for local businesses who depend upon an alienated, exploited, and dependent workforce, and profit is the end goal for multinational corporations who want to maintain or create a competitive advantage on the world stage as both employers, and the purveyors of a consumptive culture that creates markets of needs out of mountains of wants.

September 11, 2001 changed everything. The terrorist attack on American soil shifted attention from NCLB to "safety and defense in the face of the U.S. vulnerability to global terrorism" (State of New York Department of Education 2006, p. 78). NCLB marked the close of a fifty-year period of initiatives in elementary and secondary education at the federal level. The central question coming of the half-century, which proceeded NCLB, according to the State Department of Education in New York, "is how and why the federal influence has grown so dramatically in a nation whose constitution makes no reference to responsibility for education and whose practices of decentralized control of education have been presumed dominant" (p. 81).

Globalization—and the intense competition at the international level that comes with it—may explain the greater emphasis on the federal approach to a host of social issues, but especially public education. President Obama faced a number of issues when he first took office, including two wars and a crushing recession. The new administration did address education and educational spending was part of the American Recovery and Reinvestment Act. Kraft and Furlong (2013) say President Obama entered the Oval Office with an eye towards reforming NCLB.

Funds for Race to the Top were also awarded on a competitive basis to states that demonstrated how they would reform education "including the use of internationally-benchmarked standards and assessments, the recruitment and retention of effective teachers and principals, the adoption of data systems to track student progress, and the improvement of low-performing schools" (State of New York Department of Education 2006, p. 81). States were also required to have measures in place to assess teacher and administrator performance, and remove restrictions on the number of charter schools permitted in the state. Incentives for measuring teacher quality were also made available by the administration, including funds for "increased performance-based salaries for teachers and principals in high-needs schools" (p. 82).

Kraft and Furlong (2013) described the purpose of Race to Top as including promises to:

- Adopt statement learning standards and assessments;
- Build data systems to measure achievement;
- Recruit, retain, and reward effective teachers and principals through measures such as merit pay and retention bonuses;
- Foster education innovation through such means as laws encouraging charter school development;
- Focus on turning around the lowest-performing schools (p. 375).

The administration believes the federal government must drive and support change at the local and state levels where education is concerned. To that end, the administration created a model to include "assuring that all students complete high school and are prepared for college and a career, providing for great teachers and leaders in every school; creating equity and opportunity for all students; raising the bar and rewarding excellence; and promoting innovation and continuous improvement" (Kraft and Furlong 2013, p. 375).

Secretary Arne Duncan reinforced the administration's position in remarks made in 2009. Duncan describes "education as the one true path out of poverty-the great equalizer that overcomes differences in background, culture and privilege. It's the only want to secure our common future in a competitive global economy." Duncan adds, "everyone wants the best for their children and they are willing to take greater responsibility." Duncan also stated, people want support from Washington but not interference. They want accountability but not oversight. They want national leadership but not at the expense of local control."

Duncan's comments, while hopeful, assume that the playing field is level and that education miraculously lifts people out of poverty and is more of a determinant of the life chances of individuals than other factors such as race and ethnicity. Mountains of research show that racial disparities exists in terms of income, wealth, and even unemployment for blacks and whites with similar levels of education.

Americans, especially those experiencing unequal treatment, have relied on interference from Washington in address the oppressive conditions within which they have been forced to live. Similarly, historically disadvantaged groups also long for both accountability and oversight and have relied on national leadership to ensure local officials do not overstretch their authority and treat citizens as equals, which has not always been the case. It is often those with privilege and positions of authority who do not want interference or oversight.

Interestingly enough, Duncan draws from the writings of Dr. Martin Luther King, Jr.'s Letter from the Birmingham Jail to show why action must be taken on education to address racial differences in achievement exposed by NCLB. He says education is everyone's responsibility and everyone might do more. He says he needs to end the "culture of blame, self-interest and disrespect that has demeaned the field of education," which is precisely educational reform policies like NCLB have managed to accomplished. Under resourced schools are blamed from not performing as well as schools with greater resources. School choice has led to the privatization of education in many areas, especially in areas that are majority minority and related policies meet the self-interest of corporations and not the surrounding community. Schools—and the students and staff therein—must live with the stigmatization of being labeled as failing and a primary and secondary educational market is maintained which students of color relegated to schools in the secondary sector.

"Education is the civil rights issue of our generation and it can't wait—because tomorrow won't wait—the world won't wait—and our children won't wait," said Duncan. He used very progressive language, but the means used to achieve the type of educational institution imagined here are indeed regressive-turning the hands of time back in terms of forward momentum on public education.

The commitment to equity and equality in education was reinforced in comments Secretary Duncan made before the Education Writers Association Annual Conference at Vanderbilt University in Nashville, Tennessee. Duncan makes the claim that there is more outrage at the comments by former owner of the Los Angeles Clippers, Donald Sterling, than there is outrage about the current state of public education in America, namely, "our nation's achievement gaps and the fact that millions of our children still don't receive equal educational opportunity." There is outrage and the outrage has persisted, especially in minorities communities for generations and those in positions of power and privilege have sought to capitalize and exploit the issue for as long. Federal policies have—intentionally or unintentionally—contributed to the perpetuation of racial inequality in education.

Duncan also remarked, students of color don't get the same opportunity to take the courses whites and Asians take, and characterizes this as a "dummying down of expectations." We do not have a "knowledge gap" but a "courage gap and an action gap" according to Duncan. The gap that should be the focus of our attention is the gap between what we say we value and what we actually do. In the age of colorblindness, liberals often use language that point to a commitment to fairness and justice, but act in ways to the contrary.

Bonilla-Silva (2013) would likely characterize Duncan's remarks as illustrative of the abstract liberalism and minimization of racism frames of colorblind racism. Duncan uses "ideas associated with political liberalism" in abstract ways to explain racial disparities and "suggests discrimination is no longer a central factor affecting minorities' life chances," but lack of accountability, lack of responsibility, cowardice, and inaction are to blame (p. 28).

The State Department of Education in New York State highlights four trends in education over the past sixty years. The federal government has taken a greater leadership role in education and demonstrated more control over policies at the state and local levels through "legislation, regulations, and financial incentives" (p. 82). Another trend identified by the department is the shift in the use of federal aid from "attempting to redress the inequalities in education that resulted from socioeconomic disadvantage, discrimination, and language background . . . to closing achievement gaps by raising the effectiveness of education for all students" (p. 82). Another key trend is the standardization of program outcomes "for statewide, national, or international comparison" (p. 82). Lastly, the number of state coalitions advocating for changes in federal policy replaced individual states as actors.

The trends reflect a larger shift in public policy changes which are constructed within the mistaken notion that the United States is a colorblind society and therefore enacts policies that treats "everyone the same" and ignores the centuries of unequal treatment which have produced the racial disparities that persist throughout American society, including where education is concerned. As Freeman (2007) put it-in his critique of NCLB-contemporary educational policies tend to treat schooling "as a discrete domain of social inequality that dissociates educational policy from other relevant policy streams" (p. 194). Freeman further notes, "the implications of treating schools as the locus of colorblind social equality while restricting the demands we place on other public social institutions goes to the core of the debate about the authenticity of depending on legislative muscle to repair intractable racial problems" (Freeman 2007, p. 195).

Explaining racial differences in non-racial terms has become so much the norm that even those who acknowledge the existence of prejudice, discrimination, racism, sexism, and classism, continue to legislate in ways that presume that the social groups to which we belong matter only to the extent that individuals with membership in said groups fail to reach their full potential. This occurs because it is far easier to blame the victim and legislate against perceived cultural differences than to challenge structural systems and institutions which perpetually privilege some groups and disadvantages others. In other words, it is far easier to blame students, teachers, and administrators for not meeting arbitrary benchmarks than it is to acknowledge that we live within a social structure that was created for the purpose of benefiting a few at the expense of the many and one manifestation of that hierarchical racialized system is the relegation of people of color to the very bottom of the social ladder, and the use of the operation of social institutions, such as the educational system, to keep them there en mass. The emphasis on testing is illustrative of these points.

Data from the standardized tests taken in elementary and high schools show racial differences persist in a variety of contexts. Logan found that on average blacks attend elementary schools in where the reading scores are in the 35th percentile and math scores are in the 36th percentile. Whites attend elementary schools where the reading scores are in the 60th percentile in reading and in the 59th percentile in math. Blacks fared about the same in the middle and high schools. On average, blacks attended middle schools with reading and math scores in the 36th percentile, while whites attended middle schools with reading and math scores in the 61st percentile. The average black student attended a high school where the reading scores were in the 38th percentile and the math scores were in the 36th percentile. Whites attended high schools where the reading and math scores were in the 61st percentile. The gap was the greatest between schools attended by black and white students and the smallest between Asians and whites. Average test scores on reading and math was actually higher in schools Asians attended than schools attended by the average white student.

Test scores varied by race, school poverty and metropolitan location in elementary, according to John Logan's research. Logan separated the schools into high, medium, and poor categories and city, suburban, and non-metro. The gap between blacks and whites on reading in city schools was 10.9, 12.1 in the suburbs, and 10.5 in non-metro areas in schools where more than 55 percent of students were poor. The black-white gap on mathematics was 11.4 in city schools, 12.5 in suburban schools, and 11.1 in non-metro schools. The gap was higher between blacks and whites on math than on reading and higher in the suburbs than in all other areas.

The racial gap between the reading and math test scores were smaller in elementary schools where school poverty was between 25 and 55 percent. The black-white gap on reading in city schools was 5.3 and 5.7 in suburban elementary schools. The reading scores for schools attended by black students in non-metro areas were slightly higher than the reading scores for whites students in non-metro areas with medium school poverty. The test scores for schools whites were in the 53rd percentile and the test scores for schools blacks were in were in the 54th percentile. The racial gap between blacks and whites on math were about the same for reading in schools with medium poverty.

In low poverty schools the average white student in city schools attend schools where the reading scores are in the 79th percentile. Similar black students attend schools where the reading scores are in the 66th percentile.

The racial gap between blacks and whites in suburban schools on reading is 4.7 and in non-metro schools the black-white ratio for reading in elementary schools is 3.2. The black-white difference on math test scores in city schools was slightly higher than the reading scores. The racial gap in suburban schools in math is 5 and 4 in non-metro areas.

Based upon his research, Logan concludes, "these data show that racial inequalities in education are large and deeply entrenched in society. When the typical black, Hispanic, and Native American children are assigned to schools that perform so much below the median, few can be in above-average schools and a substantial share attend schools well below the 30th percentile. Attaching this pattern by focusing on a few low-achieving schools (NCLB's policy to close failing schools at the very bottom of the distribution) can have only marginal results" (Logan 2010, p. 10).

Logan says there must be changes in segregation of schools by race and class, but the issue is not a public policy priority. Logan also argues that trends in residential segregation are not likely to move more black children into more diverse neighborhood schools. Logan concludes, "Since progress in school desegregation has come to a halt in most parts of the country, partly due to the strong boundaries between school districts, and court rulings are creating obstacles to existing desegregation plans, there is little chance for improvement from this source. Efforts at equalization of poverty rates across schools, which could make a strong contribution, will also run up against the barrier of district boundaries. Decades after the *Brown v. Board of Education* desegregation order, separate and unequal continues to be the pattern in American public education (Logan 2010, p. 12).

"Race is the social expression of power and privilege" (Freeman 2005, p. 190). Race permeates every social institution in America, including public schools. The education of people of color has always been politically contested in this country and today is no different. Education has been withheld from people of color as a means of maintaining white privilege and dominance in our society and the practice was enforced with the full faith and confidence of the law. Public policies and private practices maintained the racialized social structure then, as it does now. Despite legislative gains and greater access to public education over the past few decades, the role of race in education and the role of education in the lives of people of color have changed little. People of color, particularly blacks, continue to have limited access to a quality education. Their misery continues to bring profits for those in positions to gain from it. While policymakers espouse the virtue of educational reform, especially school choice, as a means for addressing persistent racial inequality, the decisions they make to little to bring about greater equity or equality in education. Instead, the policies further the interest of the most privileged among us and maintain a racialized hierarchical system where disadvantaged whites find themselves articulating cultural explanations to account for differences between themselves and people of color and pay little attention to their own exploitation at the hands of those focused primarily on profit. In the next chapter I examine education as a profit machine.

Chapter Three

Education as a Profit Machine

Much has been written about the political economy of place and the city as a growth machine (Lyons 2009; Molotch 1993). Logan and Molotch (1987) made the argument in their oft-cited book, *Urban Fortunes,* that place is a commodity that generates power for its owners and that while elites may disagree on many things, they speak in one voice when it comes to the issue of growth. The purpose of local government and the very meaning of what constitutes a community are centered on growth. Increasingly, American public schools can be viewed in much the same way. Education is a commodity and control over public education, one of the few areas of public life that is not fully privatized, enhances the wealth and power of elites. In this chapter I examine Logan and Molotch's (1987) research on the city as a growth machine and critiques of their work. Next, I detail how the concepts identified in their research can be applied to public schools in America. Then, I focus on the various ways in which elites profit from control over public schools by focusing on linkages between public schools and the prison-industrial complex.

THE URBAN GROWTH MACHINE

Logan and Molotch (1987) offered a critique of sociological research on urban areas prior to the mid-1980s. The authors observed that there were very few discussions in the literature where place was understood as a market commodity. Commodities are goods or materials bought and sold as an article of commerce. Fuels and metals are examples of commodities. Understanding place as a market commodity explains why some individuals take an interest, or believe they have a stake, in the ordering of urban life.

The key questions surrounding research on urban life typically begin with the word who. "Who governs? (or Who rules?) (Logan and Molotch 1987, p. 50). The more important question, which Logan and Molotch (1987) describe as "the equally central question" is "For what?" (Logan and Molotch 1987, p. 50). Elites are engaged in urban life because "the city is a growth machine, one that can increase aggregate rents and trap related wealth for those in the right position to benefit" (Logan and Molotch 1987, p. 50). Logan and Molotch (1987) added that the desire for growth is the motivation behind the answers to the questions or urban life that begin with what, how, and where.

The reach of elites is quite widespread, argued Logan and Molotch (1987). Elites control public agendas-determining what, when, and how issues are addressed. The issues that make it on to the public agenda "do so precisely because they are matters on which elites have, in effect, agreed to disagree" (Logan and Molotch 1987, p. 51). Not only are elites focused almost exclusively on growth, but elites also consider growth, almost always, good. The focus of elites on what happens within a given city reverberates outward to other areas and influences growth in surround areas too. "The activism of entrepreneurs is, and always has been, a critical force in shaping the urban system, including the rise and fall of given places" (Logan and Molotch 1987, p. 52).

The use of cities as growth machines was not a new phenomenon in the mid-1980. Logan and Molotch (1987) cited historic examples to support their claim that the growth machine has been a potent force in urban development in the United States for centuries. The mudding of the waters and the blurring of the boundaries between "public and private prosperity" has been a vital part of American history (Logan and Molotch 1987, p. 53). Logan and Molotch (1987) described how city builders and the founders of early American towns used their financial, human, social, and even political capital to profit from place. Communities competed for government land, institutions of higher learning, and even prisons in the hopes of stimulating growth. Although the competition appeared to be between various individuals, in reality, the competitions were between places and were largely driven by elites focused on growth. While the individuals who came to symbolize the development of towns and cities across America were often remembered as visionaries and risk takers (Logan and Molotch 1987). "These urban founders were in the business of manipulating place for its exchange values. Their occupations most often were real estate or banking" and the "professional roles became sidelines" and "had a new unimportance" (Logan and Molotch 1987, p. 54). Historically, there has been a "tendency to use land and government activity to make money," rendering most other pursuits insignificant, and the tendency endures (Logan and Molotch 1987, p. 55).

While growth machines persist the strategies employed may change over time. Efforts to promote growth are more covert than in the past, according to

Logan and Molotch (1987). The public and the courts are less tolerant of efforts to "manipulate space and redistribute rents" than in the past (Logan and Molotch 1987, p. 57). To create greater social distance between the processes and the benefactors of the urban growth machines, elites delegated some functions to the media, policymakers, and urban professionals. The modern growth machine "has become instead a multifaceted matrix of important social institutions pressing along complementary lines" (Logan and Molotch 1987, p. 58). Today's growth machines are concerned with expanding the wealth of the elite and readily oppose anything that might threatened that end. The most important thing for elites is growth and the profits generated, which require communicating messages that link growth and a better quality of life for the masses.

To ensure a continuous emphasis on growth elites work to maintain and strengthen relationships between themselves and other important actors, especially elected officials. Mobilizing efforts to promote growth is contingent upon action by government, so "local growth elites play a major role in electing local politicians" (Logan and Molotch 1987, p. 63). The interdependent relationship between local growth elites and elected officials is understudied and often goes undetected for two reasons, said Logan and Molotch (1987). The social issues that garner the largest headlines are often the least significant to the growth agenda. Second, the issues that matter most to the urban growth machine are not as sensational and are treated by the media as dull and insignificant. Logan and Molotch (1987) detailed the roles of important players, including: politicians, local media, and organized labor. "The growth machine will sustain only certain persons as politicians" and therefore, provides the financial backing for selected candidates (Logan and Molotch 1987, p. 66). Politicians may be effective in addressing the social issues that are of the greatest importance to them, but politicians are supported based upon their ability to serve as a means to an end-growth.

Local media play an important role, according to Logan and Molotch (1987) in promoting growth for growths sake. Urban newspapers are often owned by a local business and the success of the paper is dependent upon circulation, which increases as an area experiences growth. "Its critical interest is not in the specific pattern of that growth" (Logan and Molotch 1987, p. 70). Labor unions also have an interest in growth and may function as partners in the urban growth machine. Union representatives are recruited as they are seen as impartial and poster children for "value-free development" (Logan and Molotch 1987, p. 81). Despite very visible tensions between workers and capitalists, Logan and Molotch (1987) argue that unions are used by elites and cannot of their own volition influence development.

Logan and Molotch (1987) concluded their discussion of urban growth machines with an examination of the consequences of growth. Although the champions of growth see all growth as good, the reality is that growth may be positive and negative (Molotch 1976). Growth can have mixed effects on the overall fiscal health, employment, job and income mobility, and even the environment. Growth machines can increase public expenditures, redistribute existing jobs, and depress wages and limit opportunities for upward mobility.

CRITIQUES OF THE URBAN GROWTH MACHINE

Although Logan and Molotch's (1987) book is among the most widely cited in urban sociology, the book is not without it critics. Hall and Hall (1994) focus not only on the answer to the question "for what," but also "how and why" growth and redevelopment might occur, particularly in places like Detroit, Michigan and other "declining older cities" (Hall and Hall 1994, p. 80). The researchers found that even in declining cities where growth is not occurring, "corporations have successfully and overtly used local government to facilitate corporate efforts to sustain localized economic investment" (Hall and Hall 1994, p. 88).

Lyons (2009) offered a critique of the urban growth model in his published work on eminent domain. Lyons (2009) argued that the distinctions between exchange and use values are not as clear as Logan and Molotch (1987) portrayed in their work. The model also leads to "the romanticization of residential use values" and fails to account for the negative issues that may arise from residential uses (Lyons 2009, p. 294). Moreover, Lyons (2009) said use values may not always be enhanced as set forth in the urban growth model, but use values may also be diminished, thus Logan and Molotch (1987) do not adequately consider the role of negative externalities. Lyons (2009) did say that there were two key takeaways from Logan and Molotch (1987) work that could be applied to legal debates regarding eminent domain: 1. Intensifying land use has victims and 2. Individual decisions about development pales in comparison to "the lattice of interlocking use values between parcels" (Lyons 2009, p. 295).

Kirkpatrick and Smith (2011) invited researchers to revisit the utility of the urban growth machine model, particularly during harsh economic times. Kirkpatrick and Smith (2011) said harsh economic times can have an impact on the effectiveness of growth machines.

There is an ongoing tension in education that is akin to the ongoing tension described by Logan and Molotch (1987) and others. The tension is not so much between exchange and use values; rather, the tension is between those who view education as a revolutionary and empowering extension of civic engagement and seek to challenge the status quo and those who view education as workforce development, a pipeline to prison, and a bridge to benefits, and wish to maintain the status quo. Much like the urban growth machine, local media and politicians play key roles in the current state of public schools in America. Local media are the mouthpiece of the privileged. Media dictates not only what is newsworthy, but also how various stories are represented. The media's role is not to communicate to those directly impacted by decisions made with respect to public education; rather, the role of the media is to communicate to the larger society, and the message communicated seeks to maintain the privileged positions of elites. Elected officials, even the most well-meaning among them, cannot expect to maintain their political positions without the support and backing from individuals with wealth, status, and power. Thus, elected officials may at times find themselves crossing the aisle on selected issues. These issues often appear politically neutral. Bipartisanship occurs much more frequently on issues that benefit the elite most and partisan impasses are much more likely on issues elites could not care less about. In terms of education we find bipartisan support for educational reform, which benefits elites and partisan disagreements as to how best to bring about the stated reform. Thus, the dialogue is not about the system and how it functions to benefit some and hurt others; the dialogue is instead centered around how parents, students, teachers, administrators, and community leaders will ensure that reform takes place and the victims of the system take the blame not only for the need for reform but for standing in the way of reform. The role of elites in creating crises and structures to create chaos and misery for their own benefit is rarely a topic of public conversation and when such issues are raised, messengers are often discredited and movements aimed at bringing about social change are repressed.

Logan and Moltoch (1987) were critiqued for failing to adequately account for an apparent absence of growth in old and deteriorating cities and during financial crisis. I argue that it is precisely in these times when education as a growth machine is most evident. In areas that may be described as distressed or deteriorated or in the midst of an economic crisis, the fiscal pain is felt in schools. Schools in these areas are under resourced and are largely majority minority schools due to such things as residential segregation, white flight, and other forms of resistance to court mandated desegregation. Soon there is an investment in for-profit schools and/or the creation of magnet schools and gifted and talented programs, which resegregate students by forcing ill-prepared students to maintain grades without the support they need. These students are disproportionately student of color and these students soon find themselves sent to the limited number of remaining neighborhood-based schools, many of which are under resourced and/or are deemed as failing by state and national standards. After the magnet and other specialized public schools are purged of most students of color, working- and middle-class white students return.

The return of working- and middle-class whites to old deteriorating and distressed areas is well documented in the literature on gentrification (Drew

2012; Hwang and Sampson 2014). A recent study by researchers at Harvard revealed that gentrification is more likely to occur in some areas than in others (Hwang and Sampson 2014). Specifically, the scholars found that if the black population exceeds 40 percent, gentrification is not as likely as in areas where the black population is smaller. What we have here are what I call "post-racial gentrifiers." These individuals consider themselves to be quite progressive. They articulate a commitment to fairness, justice, equality, and to diversity, but at the same time these individuals are not likely to see their own privilege and the continued disadvantaged position of people of color. Post-racial gentrifiers see race relations as "better than they used to be" and may even believe that their presence in the changing neighborhood is evidence of their own commitment to liberalism (Bonilla-Silva 2013). In the end post-racial gentrifiers believe racism exists, but it exists largely without racists, with the exception of a few highly profiled cases, such as those with membership in hate groups or individuals like Donald Sterling who make racially charged comments when they think the world is not listening (Bonilla-Silva 2013, Martin 2013).

Investments into selected public schools also return when whites return and are accompanied by efforts to redevelop areas of the old deteriorating and distressed areas with an eye toward attracting families with membership in the dominant racial group, many of whom have school-aged children, or work for the public school system, or local and state government. What is left is a two-sector public education system that feeds into two-sector labor market. The two-sector public education system is made up of schools in the primary sector where students are not members of a historically disadvantaged racial or ethnic group, and where schools have adequate resources and enrichment activities. The secondary sector of the public education system includes the under resourced schools, which are majority minority. Both sectors are expected to meet the same state and nationally imposed standards.

The primary sector of the labor market is one to which students in the primary sector of the public education system have access. It is here that graduates of the primary sector of the public education system will eventually find jobs, especially after completing some college or earning a college degree, for which they were prepared for throughout their high school careers. The secondary sector of the labor market is comprised of low wage, dead-end jobs, that seldom offer benefits and these are the kinds of jobs that are in the future of students in the secondary sector of the public education system. Students who do not earn a high school diploma may end up chronically unemployed and involved in the underground economy, or in the custody of the state.

PATHWAYS TO PROSPERITIES:
THE SCHOOL-TO-PRISON PIPELINE

The Criminalization of Blackness

The marginalization of black youth in the secondary sector of the public school market, involves the criminalization of blacks in general, and black students in particular. The school-to-prison pipeline is not a myth. It is very real. Wilson (2014) described the school-to-prison pipeline as "the causal link between educational exclusion and criminalization of youth" (p. 49). Several scholars have written about the criminalization of youth (Blakenship and Blankenship 2014). The treatment of young people in the juvenile justice system in Kentucky is indicative of what is happening in courts across the nation where young people are thrust into a system for offenses based mainly on their age. Victor Rios (2006) aptly described the linkages between education, the labor market, the welfare state, and the criminal justice system as the "youth control complex."

Events such as those surrounding the killings of Trayvon Martin and Michael Brown are the subject of quite a bit of recent work on the criminalization of black youth, however the criminalization of black males is not new and is not restricted to young people. Johnson (2004) wrote about the history of the criminalization of blacks in Philadelphia, Pennsylvania, and in the broader society. Johnson (2004) focused on the post-World War II era as the period when incarceration was used as a form of controlling the black populations—a population many whites, including those in law enforcement, feared and stereotyped. In fact, Johnson (2004) argued that whites considered blacks to be "criminals" and "social outcasts." Racial tensions between blacks and whites during the period following World War II were high and law enforcement officials were often called to intervene. According to Johnson (2004), officers tended to side with whites. Black residents reported brutality and harassment at the hands of white police officers. While some white police officers turn a blind eye and a deaf ear to illegal gambling and prostitution, they regularly harassed law-abiding citizens. These tensions caused a lack of trust between black residents and the predominately white law enforcement officials in their areas. Additionally, Johnson (2004) recorded how law enforcement officials were used to enforce racial discrimination. In many cities, including Philadelphia, blacks were excluded from public spaces. Swimming pools were one of the places blacks could not enjoy, even when their tax dollars helped to maintain them. Johnson (2004) writes that blacks learned to rely on activists and historically black institutions for help and not law enforcement. Most importantly, Johnson's (2004) research found that the unequal treatment received by black residents in Philadelphia during the post-war period was not tied to an increase or decrease in crime rates.

The criminalization of black residents has taken on different forms in more contemporary times. Arnold (1990) wrote about the victimization of black women and the processes of criminalization. Arnold (1990) interviewed incarcerated black women and found out that almost all of the subjects in the study faced gender oppression, economic oppression, and discrimination in the public school system. The women were sexually abused in their homes, which led them to run away from home and running away led some to be charged as vagrants or as truants. Some women reported stealing food to survive or selling their bodies to make ends meet. The women reported attending schools where they were alienated and oppressed, which caused some to dropout. Arnold (1990) described this as structural dislocation. Structural dislocation occurs when one is removed-voluntarily and/or involuntarily-from a social institution and reassociation with the institution is not likely due to the reason the removal occurred in the first place. The women in the study were removed from two critical institutions, two of three institutions Franklin (2007) described as anchor institutions in the black community: the family and the school.

In addition to the victimization and criminalization of black women who become status offenders, there are other ways in which blacks are criminalized, especially by tactics that appear apolitical and devoid of racial overtones. Civil gang injunctions and tactics, such as stop-and-frisk, on the surface appear race-neutral. Each strategy is aimed at ensuring public safety, which most rational-minded individuals support. However, civil gang injunctions and stop-and-frisk like initiatives provide some of the best evidence of the significance of race in America. Together the longer term acceptance of stop-and-frisk (and similar programs) and civil gang injunctions, point to the unwillingness on the part of members of the dominant group to accept certain individuals with minority group status, in this case, poor blacks. Civil gang injunctions and stop-and-frisk like tactics, which would likely not be tolerated in predominately white communities, are classic examples of the manifestations of racism in the 21st century.

In a guide for prosecutors published by Max Shiner, Deputy City Attorney, City of Los Angeles, California, on behalf of the National District Attorney's Association, the purpose of the civil gang injunctions was outlined. Shiner (2009) acknowledged the use of civil injunctions to fight gang crime was unconventional. In fact, Shiner (2009) stated, "this use of civil injunction law is certainly an expansion of the traditional purview of prosecutors, existing law in most jurisdictions" (Shiner, 2009:1). The guide was meant to identify some common challenges to the injunctions for prosecutors in other localities.

Injunctions, wrote Shiner (2009) were typically associated with "trifling annoyances" and "nuisances" (Shiner 2009, p. 3). Historically, civil injunctions were used to address public health, such as "in the case of keeping diseased animals or the maintenance of a pond breeding malarial mosquitoes" (Shiner 2009, p. 3). Civil injunctions, historically, also addressed public safety issues "as in the case of the storage of explosives in the midst of the city or the shooting of fireworks in the public streets" (Shiner 2009, p. 3). In each case, "the interferences with the public right were so unreasonable that it was held to constitute a criminal offense" (Shiner 2009, p. 3).

People of color, particularly black males, are seen in much the same way, as public nuisances, as threats to public health and public safety. While the term "public" seems inclusive, it could best be understood as a colorblind term for white. Race thinkers have long pondered what it means to be a problem (DuBois 1903). The targeting of largely minority communities through civil gang injunctions is one of the latest iterations of the view of people of color as inassimilable and as perpetual others.

It is not a coincidence that civil gang injunctions originated in Los Angeles where the police department has a history of troubled relations with communities of color, before, and after, the infamous beating of Rodney King. Muniz's (2014) work on civil gang injunctions showed that in some cases civil gang injunctions occurred in places where there was not a lot of crime, but where black communities were close to white, middle, and upper class areas. Civil gang injunctions in such areas capitalize on a fear of crime and provide support for theories, such as the broken window theory, which holds that smaller crimes create a climate for worse crimes (Harcourt 1998). Muniz (2014) concluded that civil gang injunctions criminalize individuals and entire groups. Like the Black Codes of old, civil gang injunctions "criminalize a broad range of mundane activities within the targeted community" (p. 219). A closer examination of injunctions highlights the criminalization of everyday activities under civil gang injunctions, which are more likely to impact individuals and communities of color.

California statutes define public nuisance in such a way that "any criminal street gang's harmful activities fall within at least one" of four categories (Shiner 2009, p. 6). The following constitutes a nuisance in California:

1. Anything which is injurious to health;
2. Anything which is indecent or offensive to the senses;
3. Anything which is an obstruction to the free use of property so as to interfere with the comfortable enjoyment of life or property;
4. Anything which unlawfully obstructs the free passage of use, in the customary manner, of any navigable lake, or river, bay, stream, canal, or basin, or any public park, square, street, or highway (Shiner 2009, p. 6).

Furthermore, the California Civil Code section 3480 defines "public nuisance" as "one which affects an entire community or neighborhood, or any considerable number of persons, although the extent of the annoyance of damage inflicted upon individuals may be unequal" (Shiner 2009, p. 6).

Civil gang injunctions, from a policy standpoint, stigmatize people of color, particularly young males of color, as a problem and extends those characterizations to the neighborhoods in which they live and anyone within the geographic area that they may come into contact with. Ironically, the areas impacted by an injunction are called a safety zone, although many of the residents do not feel safe; rather, many residents in the targeted zones feel as though they are under siege.

The requirements for obtaining an injunction are among the most generous our society has seen in some time. Prosecutors must show "that the traditional legal remedy is inadequate" (Shiner 2009, p. 9), which some in law enforcement do not see as an obstacle "because an ordinary damage award will not make a community whole for the harm the gang's activities cause" (Shiner 2009, p. 9). To that end, gang injunctions can prohibit gang members to drive, stand, sit, walk, gather, or appear in public with any known gang member. The nature and quality of such associations is not relevant. Gang members must follow the do not associate order, or face arrest. Gang members, even gang members twenty-one-years of age and older must stay away from alcohol and obey curfew.

Individuals affected by a gang injunction may not possess an open container of an alcoholic beverage, or "knowingly remaining in the presence of anyone possessing an open container of an alcoholic beverage, or knowingly remaining in the presence of an open container of an alcoholic beverage." (Shiner 2009, p. 9). Moreover, gang members many not be outside between 10:00 pm and 5:00 am, without a legitimate reason.

Precisely what makes someone a gang member remains unknown. According to a 2010 *New York Times* report, "legally there is no single definition. To be considered a gang member under state law, a law enforcement official trained in gangs must 'validate' membership by determining that a person falls under at least two criteria from a list that includes self-admission of gang affiliation, frequenting a gang area, gang dress and tattoos, and using hand signs associated with gangs" (Wollan 2010). Jory Steele, an attorney with the American Civil Liberties Union, is quoted as saying, "Gang injunctions function like roving warrants, and they can lead to a lot of racial profiling." The burden of proving one is not a gang member is quite difficult. Individuals "must prove that he has had no association with suspected gang members for three years" (Wollan 2010).

The potential impact on families could be quite disastrous. Civil gang injunctions have the potential to remove hundreds more people of color from their communities and any opportunities to accumulate assets, but civil gang injunctions may further exacerbate the family. Individuals identified as gang members may have family members in the "safety zone" with whom they can no longer associate. Family members are fearful law enforcement will declare them guilty by association.

Opposition to the civil gang injunctions is not only growing, but is enjoying some success. A nearly $30 million class-action lawsuit was filed against Los Angeles over the use of curfews in the injunctions. "The federal lawsuit filed in 2011 alleges the city's use of curfews to limit the movements of alleged gang members inside the injunction areas is vague and a violation of the Constitution" (Charles 2013). A civil rights attorney "compares gang inunction curfews to sundown laws, which once barred people of color from being in majority-white cities after dark." Olu Orange, the attorney bringing the suit remarked, "They took the concept of sundown town that used to cover other people's towns and dropped it on these neighborhoods. In the sundown town, they said, 'Don't let us catch you outside in our town after sundown.' Now, it's 'Don't let us catch you outside in your own town after sundown'" (Charles 2013).

A number of young people report stops by Los Angeles Police Department officers. Once it was confirmed some young boys were not on the gang injunction list, several were still cited for violating other minor offenses (e.g., violating the curfew in effect for all minors, not just those on the injunction list). Evidence of the effectiveness of civil gang injunctions is mixed. Grogger (2002) found violent crimes decreased 5–10 percent in the years after the injunctions were introduced, but at the same time, Grogger observed, "in comparison with these other place-based enforcement efforts, the effects of the gang injunctions are relatively small" (Grogger 2002, p. 88).

While opponents of civil gang injunctions raise concerns about violations of the right to assembly and the right to equal protection, opponents of stop and frisk and similar tactics were concerned about violations of the Fourth Amendment. Theodore Souris addressed some of the early concerns in the mid-1960s in response to comments made in support of top and frisk by Dr. Herbert L. Packer. Souris (1966) begins his remarks, published in *The Journal of Criminal Law, Criminology and Police Science*, saying, "all thoughtful citizens must concede (Stop and Frisk) presents a conflict between individual liberty and effective police procedures" (Souris 1966, p. 251). Souris (1966) adds, "free men should no more be subject to having the police run their hands over their pockets than through them. Neither the Fourth Amendment nor, for that matter, the common law of tort distinguishes as does the majority between a cursory search and a more elaborate one. In both instances, it is the slightest touch which is condemned, and the reason for this is that the insult to individuality, to individual liberty, is as grave and as objectionable in the one case as in the other" (Souris 1996, p. 260). He called upon law enforcement and scholars to consider other strategies for combating crime "which do not require that we tamper with the most fundamental of our constitutional rights as citizens, our right to be free" (Souris 1996 p. 262).

Souris's (1966) sentiments are both echoed, and challenged, in more contemporary times. Starkey (2012) finds that showing the discriminatory intent, in many contexts, became virtually impossible with the Supreme Court's decision in the matter of *Personnel Administrator of Massachusetts v. Feeney*. The case, which dealt with gender discrimination, "held that absent a discriminator purpose, a facially neutral law does not violate equal protection violation" (Starkey 2012, p. 151). Starkey (2012) finds that the *Feeney* case, as well as other cases, results in "a more salient problem . . . a governmental actor can always deny that racial animus played any role in decision making" (Starkey 2012, p. 151).

The evidence was quite clear that people of color were disproportionately impacted by stop-and-frisk. Data analyses performed by the New York Police Department and civil liberty groups regularly showed the disproportionate impact of stop-and-frisk on communities of color, and on black males in particular.

Despite the popularity of civil gang injunctions and stop-and-frisk like programs, these approaches to fighting crime fall short of achieving stated goals. For example, a recent report from the Attorney General's Office in New York State found that half of stop-and-frisk arrests did not lead to convictions; rather, increased the number of young black and Hispanic males involved in the criminal justice system, which places these young men at greater risk of incarceration in the future. "Stop-and-frisk has been around for decades, but its use grew dramatically under Mayor Michael Bloomberg's administration to an all-time high in 2011 of 684,330 stops, mostly of black and Hispanic men. To make a stop, police must have reasonable suspicion that a crime is about to occur or has occurred, a standard lower than the probable cause needed to justify an arrest. Only about 10 percent of the stops result in arrests or summonses, and weapons are found about 2 percent of the times" (CBSNewYork/AP November 14, 2013).

More specifically, the report from the Attorney General's Office found that less than 2 percent of stop-and-frisk arrests led to the incarceration of an individual for more than a month. Of the 1.5 percent of stop-and-frisk arrest that lead to incarceration of longer than thirty days, "a tenth of 1 percent led to convictions for weapons charges or violent crimes" (CBSNew York/AP November 14, 2013). Donna Liberman with the New York Civil Liberties Union summarized the findings this way, "The numbers stand as stark evidence that this stop-and-frisk program is not about keeping our streets safe; it's certainly about putting people-people of color primarily-into the criminal justice system" (CBSNew York/AP November 14, 2013). Seemingly color-blind policies such as civil gang injunctions and stop-and-frisk, which current New York City Mayor DeBlasio campaigned to end, have the intended, or unintended consequence, of placing for people of color at-risk for incarceration and locked up and locked out of the wealth accumulation process.

Mychal Denzel Smith, writing for *The Nation,* discussed the normative practice of criminalizing young people of color not only on American streets, but in schools too. Smith cited the case of seven-year old Rodrigo Diaz who was handcuffed by police and interrogated for an incident on the playground over $5 as just one example of "a daily routine." Our society, argued Smith, creates "these images of monsters and then wonder why people go out slaying" young people of color, like Rodrigo Diaz, Trayvon Martin and Jordan Davis.

Dr. David J. Leonard commented on the criminalization of black youth in American public schools in a piece appearing in *Urban Cusp.* He argued that the police department, George Zimmerman's attorney, and the media sought to justify the killing of Trayvon Martin by portraying the shooting victim as "a criminal, as a thug and as a menace." He summarized the efforts of the three entities as "the blame the black kid defense." Diverting public attention away from Zimmerman and issues surround his culpability, the Sanford Police, Zimmerman's attorney, and some in the media focused instead on Trayvon Martin's posts on social media, school records, and physical appearance, including wearing a hooded sweatshirt. The emphasis placed on Martin's school records "reveals the ways that profiling and his criminalization began long before Zimmerman." Leonard (2012) summarized the treatment of black youth as follows, "black youth are demonized, denied access to a worthwhile educational experience, and funneled from locked down schools to places of incarceration all while the likes of Zimmerman guard gated communities from the intrusion of the unwanted." Black youth are the poster children for the unwanted in society, especially young black males.

The criminalization of black students is related to zero tolerance and disciplinary strategies in schools particularly in majority minority schools.

Zero Tolerance and the Discipline Gap

According to Wilson (2014), schools contribute to the prison population with half of individuals entering correction facilities earned a high school diploma or graduation equivalency diploma. The fear of black youth in particular, brought on by concerns over violent and drug-related crimes, led not only to the criminalization of black youth, but it also led to the adoption of zero-tolerance policies in schools. Schools, said Wilson (2014), "adopted the same strategies as courts and seek to remove students who problematic behavior gets in the way of learning. Harsh disciplinary procedures, school-based officers, mandatory reporting of behavioral incidents, and the use of school exclusion as a punishment have become common place" (p. 50). While national crime trends have gone down, Wilson (2014) cited a report from the

Office of Juvenile Justice and Delinquency Prevention (OJJD) showing the number of school referrals to police and juvenile justice have gone up.

Dahlberg (2012) found an increase in the use of police to enforce student codes of conduct, which have led to the arrest of young people of color in schools. In places like Massachusetts, far too many students of color were charged in recent years with disturbing a lawful assembly for talking back to teachers and school administrators, for example. Dahlberg (2012) found that students were arrested for problems such as "bringing cell phones and Ipods to school, smoking cigarettes, and skipping class." NYCLU summarized the issue as follows,

> The over-policing of New York City schools, paired with school zero toler-ance policies, drives youth directly towards the juvenile and criminal justice systems. While the city over-invests in expensive policing measures for schools that are disproportionately low income, black and Latino, these schools remain under-resourced in fundamental areas that harm student learn-ing (Pownall 2013).

Racial differences in disciplinary action in public schools describes the discipline gap (Arcia 2007, Booker and Mitchell 2011, Gregory and Weinstein 2008, Skiba et al. 2011).

Data from the U.S. Department of Education Office for Civil Rights (2014) showed the severity of the discipline gap. While black children represented 18 percent of preschool enrollment, black children represented almost half of preschool children with more than one out-of-school suspension. The report also showed that black students were three times as likely as white students to be suspended and expelled. Although boys are suspended and expelled at a much higher rate than girls, black girls are suspended at much higher rates than girls with membership in any other racial or ethnic group and most boys. Moreover, "while black students represent 16 percent of student enrollment, they represent 27 percent of students referred to law enforcement and 31 percent of students subjected to a school-related arrest. In comparison, white students represent 51 percent of enrollment, 41 percent of students referred to law enforcement, and 39 percent of those arrested." Students with disabilities who are disproportionately black had high rates of seclusion and involuntary confinement.

According to the U.S. Department of Education's (2014) findings, some states are faring better in terms of discipline, restraint, and seclusion. Black males had the highest out-of-school suspensions of male students by race/ethnicity for the 2011–2012 school year, with the exception of Montana, where American Indian/Alaska Natives had the highest out-of school suspensions of male students. Black females had the highest percentages of out-of-school suspensions for all female students nationally, but Idaho, Maine, Mississippi, Montana, Rhode Island, South Dakota, and Vermont were exceptions.

Zero tolerance policies feed the school-to-prison pipeline. Zero tolerance "requires that certain behaviors are immediately punished, without considering the circumstances or seeking the student's perspective. Under zero tolerance, a student who talks back to a teacher may receive the same swift punishment as a student who brings drugs or a weapon to school" (Dahlberg 2013, p. 9).

Dahlberg (2008) published an earlier report on how discretionary school discipline contributes to the school-to-prison pipeline. Under the Bloomberg Administration the total number of annual suspensions doubled compared to ten years earlier. According to the report, there were about 30,000 annual suspensions in 2001 and about 70,000 in 2011. While blacks students made up less than a third of the public school population, black students represented half of all suspensions during the 2012-2011 academic year compared to white students who made up 14 percent of the public school population, but only 7 percent of students suspended. Dahlberg's (2008) report also showed that whites were more likely to be suspended for objective disciplinary acts and blacks were more likely to be suspended for subjective disciplinary acts. Additionally, the research uncovered that more than 60 percent of all school arrests in New York City involved black students.

The criminalization of the classroom has led to the incarceration of students directly and indirectly (Dahlberg 2008). In New York, the increase in school-arrests occurred after then Mayor Rudolph Giuliani pressured the Board of Education to turn over school security to the New York City Police Department in 1996.

The criminalization of the classroom is not only an issue in NewYork, but it is an epidemic nationally. In a statement for the Department of Justice, Melodee Hanes (2012) of the Office of Juvenile Justice and Delinquency Prevention Office of Justice Programs addressed the need to end the school-to-prison pipeline. Hanes (2012) cited research from her office which found that students who are suspended, expelled or arrested are more likely to be held back, not graduate or become part of the juvenile justice system. Black students, testified Hanes, were about 30 percent more likely to "receive discretionary discipline actions as compared to white and Hispanic students." Even more heartbreaking was the finding that "suspension or expulsion of a student for a discretionary violation nearly tripled the likelihood of juvenile justice contact within the subsequent academic year." Involvement with the juvenile justice system has negative effects on the child and on the system, according to Hanes. Long-term and short-term consequences for the child include not only a greater likelihood of dropping out of school, but higher unemployment, poor health, and low income over the life course. Additionally, Hanes (2012) stated that the juvenile justice system is better equipped to deal with serious offenses as opposed to school-based misconduct.

Prison Prophets

Prisons are big business, especially the privatization of prisons. One could argue that it is not a coincidence that privatization of prisons occurred around the same time as efforts to privatize public education and the mass incarceration of young black males. Corrections Corp of America (CCA) and GEO Group were identified as some of the major players in the rise of prisoners for profits. Rashad Robinson, Executive Director, ColorOfChange, addressed the proliferation of private prisons over the past few decades. In article that appeared in the *Huffington Post*, Robinson said that the number of people incarcerated in private prisons increased by more than 1000 percent. Robinson also noted, "private prison companies get to cherry pick who they imprison, and in order to cut cost and increase profit, companies choose younger and healthier people who are disproportionately Black and Latino due to the discriminatory War on Drugs of recent years. The already devastating racial disparities of the pubic prison system are even worse in private prisons."

Private prisons, argued Robinson, show little concern for the constitution and are primarily concerned with profits, of which it is estimated they generate about $5 billion a year. Efforts to eliminate private prisons, according to Robinson, are on the rise.

Fasching-Varner et al. (2014) discussed the linkages between schools and prisons in their introduction to a special issue of *Equity Excellence in Education* on the subject of the school-to-prison pipeline. The researchers included a description of the economic benefits of mass incarceration that goes beyond the profits to corporations behind private prisons. One economic benefit is that mass incarceration limits competition for valued resources. Individuals who are locked up are also locked out-they are locked out of the labor market. They are unable to acquire and amass wealth, but individuals, who tend to have membership in the dominant racial group in America, face few structural and institutional barriers to income and assets. The researchers showed, "those in prison do not simply help maintain the balance of wealth and power, they actually serve to create larger differences" (p. 416)

Fasching-Varner et al. (2014) also made the claim that there is a relationship between unemployment and incarceration. "The state adjusts incarceration practices to match the economic equilibrium within the society. In times of low unemployment less imprisonment occurs" (p. 417). Imprisonment increases when unemployment is relatively high "to absorb surplus labor and suppress social unrest associated with economic deprivation" (p.417).

Research point to the economic policies of the Regan Administration contributed to the lasting economic benefits of prisons (Fasching-Varner et al. 2014). The rich became richer and the poor became poorer. The 1980s were characterized by "leveraging crime, punishment, and incarceration as a neauveaux industry – a mechanism for wealth to replicate and for those not deemed worthy to produce more than they consume" (p. 417). The benefactors of punishment for profit were varied and included everyone from suppliers to construction companies.

Reframing the dialogue to one focused on a prison-to-school pipeline the researchers set forth the following argument:

> We do not believe that incarceration occurs simply because crime is committed or because of cracks in the schooling system. We believe that the impact of prisons opens our vision to seeing that prisons demand a clientele, particularly given the relative economic instability over the last 35 years, save some time in the mid 1990's, which requires prisons, as previously mentioned, to regulate unemployment and create financial separation between races, ethnicities and socio-economic groups. Prisons, which are increasingly privatized, do not simply meet society's demand for a space to execute punishment, they in fact create an entire enterprise, and a well-lobbied one, whose base function rallies around having a population to punish. Without that population the economic equilibrium is threatened as more people have a need for employment that would otherwise be locked up, and the prison profiteers loose serious wealth potential reality that the free-market will not allow to come to fruition (Fasching-Varner et al. 2014, p. 418).

Fasching-Varner et al. (2014), warned,

> For those looking to be profiteers from educational reform there are significant economic gains to be had from that interest – that is so long as the debt remains the services of educational reformers will be necessary, and the 'interest' paid toward the education debt materializes in real money for those in educational reform, regardless of whether or not reform actually occurs. The parallel phenomena is true of our correction systems, as discussed earlier, in terms of the profit and growth potential being better served by never addressing the principle of the debts levied against those most vulnerable in our society. That is to say, in both education and 'correction' there are more advantages, financially, to not 'fix' the problems, but help exacerbate them in order to keep the educational reformers and prison profiteers in business (p. 420).

Bridges to Benefits

The linkages between prisons and public schools and other social institutions is illustrative of what my colleagues and I called, bridges to benefits (Martin et al. 2014). We made the argument that the pipeline between schools and the prison exists because of "networks of white privilege, which flow between institutions" (Martin et al. 2004, p. 60). We developed the idea based upon the previous research on predominately white institutions and the creation and maintenance of walls that protect whiteness at institutions of higher learning and beyond. Similar to predominately whites institutions, we argued,

> correctional facilities, inner-city public schools, unemployment lines, and social services are considered Black spaces. Political rhetoric and media representations reinforce negative stereotypes about Blacks. These stereotypes include the perception that Blacks do not value education; Blacks have a propensity towards violence; and that Blacks are lazy and unmotivated and prefer to live off of public assistance than work and receive an honest day's pay (Block, Aumann, & Chelin 2012). Demographically, prisons, failing schools, and social service agencies are far too often majority Black, or are spaces where Blacks are overrepresented relative to their population in the broader society (Alexander 2012; Martinez, Banchero, & Little 2002; Monnant 2010). Prisons, schools and social service agencies are "structured in ways that reflect their historical demography, ideology, and associated hegemonies" (Brunsma et al. 2013; p. 721)" (Martin et al. 2014, p. 67).

Bridges to benefits connect individuals with membership in the dominant racial group in America with one another. Members of the dominant racial group not only protect their privilege but they also protect and reinforce the privileges of group members through their interactions with each other through various social institutions. "Under resourced schools, for example, provide the inputs for the school-to-prison pipeline" (Martin et al. 2014, p. 68).

Furthermore, "bridges to benefits rely on white privilege ideology. The unwillingness to see or to concede that whites receive unearned benefits allows whites in positions of power and influence the cover to continue to reap returns on their investments into the misery—or systematic disadvantage of Blacks—and reciprocate and enjoy those benefits across institutions" (Martin et al. 2014, p. 69).

Additionally, Martin et al. (2014) argued, whites exhibit a sense of entitlement to a quality of education in their resistance to desegregate schools and with respect to the justice system and the economy. "Whites demonstrate a sense of entitlement in efforts to privatize prisons and to locate prisons in predominately white communities where the mass incarceration of mostly Black men serves as a form of economic development" (Martin et al. 2014, p. 69).

"Whites not only receive protection from the invisible walls which protect attacks against white supremacy, but more significantly whites use their positions in social institutions to facilitate the flow of benefits associated with whiteness within and between institutions, such as education, the economy, and the law, and capitalize on the misery of Blacks while simultaneously protecting white supremacy" (Martin et al. 2014, p. 60).

The (mis)education of black students is profitable. By understanding how growth machines operate, it becomes increasingly clear how education is viewed as a commodity that generates wealth, status, and power for elites positioned to benefit from it. Control over public education is increasingly in the hands of for-profit organizations and out of the hands of individuals impacted the most. I examined Logan and Molotch's (1987) research on the city as a growth machine and critiques of their work. Next, I detailed how the concepts identified in their research can be applied to public schools in America. Then, I focused on the various ways in which elites profit from control over public schools by focusing on linkages between public schools and the prison-industrial complex. I addressed the impact of zero tolerance policies and discretionary actions, which contribute to the discipline gap in public schools. The connection between a rise in private prisons and public schools was also discussed. The chapter ended with a discussion of the ways in which individuals with membership in the dominant group benefit from their ties with other members of the dominant group in social institutions throughout the nation. In the next chapter, I examine the Wal-Mart business model and its use in public schools in America.

Chapter Four

Race, Public Education and The Wal-Mart Model

There is no shortage of research on Wal-Mart and the many ways the multinational corporation fundamentally changed the way people do business in the U.S. and abroad (Bonanno and Goetz 2012; Ellickson and Grieco 2013; Glandon and Jaremski 2014; Horwitz 2009; Madrick 2011; Walton 1992). Research on the effects of Wal-Mart's entry and expansions on local economies, workers, and communities is mixed (Wolf and Pyrroz 2014). Some research shows the presence of Wal-Mart has positive effects, while other research shows the presence of Wal-Mart has negative effects (Goez and Rupasingha 2012; Horwitz 2009; Pew Research Center 2005; Walton 1992). Nonetheless, there is a consensus that Wal-Mart stores produce some form of change. In this chapter, I examine Wal-Mart's growing presence in the United States and throughout the globe, since the day Sam Walton purchased a Ben Franklin 5 and 10 retail store in Arkansas. I also discuss important periods in the history of the corporation from the vantage point of the corporation and researchers. Next, I analyze Sam Walton's ten rules for success in business. Lastly, I explore how capitalists and others are using the hidden curriculum in Sam Walton's model in their efforts to profit from public education.

BRIEF HISTORY OF WAL-MART

According to Wal-Mart's official web site, there are over 11,000 Wal-Mart stores in twenty-seven different countries. Wal-Mart employs over two million people, which is more than the population of Houston, Texas. The average hourly wage for full-time Wal-Mart workers in 2013 was about $13.00

an hour and about $12.00 for part-time workers. Over half of Wal-Mart's employees work in the United States. Three-quarters of store management began as hourly workers and earn between $50,000 and $170,000 a year. Net sales for Wal-Mart for 2013 were $473 billion dollars.

In 2013 Wal-Mart and the Walton Family Foundation donated more than one billion dollars in cash and in-kind contributions, which amounts to about 2 percent of their overall net worth. Five of the wealthiest Americans are related to Sam Walton—four are the children of Sam Walton and the other is Walton's sister-in-law. According to Buzzfeed, as of 2012 the Walton's had more wealth than the bottom 40 percent of Americans. The Chief Executive Officer (CEO) of Wal-Mart earned a salary of $35 million in 2010. CEO Michael Duke earned more in one hour than the average full-time Wal-Mart worker earned in 365-days.

According to Daily Finance, if Wal-Mart were a country it would be the twent-sixth largest economy in the world. Sam Walton's brainchild is bigger than Home Depot, Kroger, Target, Sears, Costco, and K-Mart combined. Wal-Mart has become such an integral part of American life (and the American economy) that twenty-five percent of every dollar Americans spend on groceries is spent at Wal-Mart. The aforementioned data is not hard to believe when you know that 90 percent of Americans live within fifteen miles of a Wal-Mart.

Sam Walton got his start in retail in Arkansas. On July 2, 1962, Walton opened his first Wal-Mart in Rogers, Arkansas. In less than a decade, Walton owned twenty-four stores. By 1969, the company Sam Walton started was legally incorporated as Wal-Mart Stores, Inc. The newly formed company opened its first distribution center in Bentonville, Arkansas by 1971. A year later there were over fifty Wal-Mart stores.

Wal-Mart's corporate page describes the 1980s as a decade of firsts. At the beginning of the decade Wal-Mart became the fastest company to reach $1 billion in sales. In 1980 there were almost 300 stores and over 20,000 employees, who Wal-Mart refers to as associates. Wal-Mart opened its first Sam's Club in Oklahoma. During the 1980s Wal-Mart replaced traditional cash registers with a computerized point-of-sale system that expedited the checkout process. On the technology front, Wal-Mart also installed a satellite communication system to improve communication by linking the company's operations long before most other retail companies. Toward the end of the decade, Wal-Mart opened its first Supercenter in Missouri. Supercenters combined department stores and supermarkets.

By the 1990s, Wal-Mart firmly secured its place as one of the most dominant retailers in the country and increasingly, around the world. Wal-Mart moved to the head of the class and was the nation's number one retailer in America in 1990. Wal-Mart opened its first store outside of the United States during the same year in Mexico. In the early 1990s there were almost

2,000 Wal-Mart stores and the company employed over 370,000 people. By the mid-1990s, Wal-Mart was opening stores in China and in Canada. Never a stranger to innovation, Wal-Mart introduced the Neighborhood Market format where it all began in Arkansas. Wal-Mart closed the decade with a deal that paved the way for Wal-Mart stores to open in the United Kingdom.

Wal-Mart ushered in the twenty-first century with the launch of Walmart.com. By 2000 Wal-Mart employed over one million employees and almost 4,000 stores around the world. Wal-Mart was at the top of Fortune's 500 ranking of America's largest companies and Wal-Mart celebrated by gaining entry into the market in Japan. The first decade of the new century closed with Wal-Mart extending its reach to Chile. Soon India joined the list of countries with ties to Wal-Mart, Inc.

DOING BUSINESS THE SAM WALTON WAY

Sam Walton was born in the heartland of America in 1918. In his memoir, Walton described his humble beginnings. He showed how his father struggled during the Great Depression, along with millions of other Americans. While his father seemed to lack the drive and entrepreneurial spirit that would mark Sam Walton's life, his mother seemed to have an abundance of it. Walton's mother started a milk business during the Depression and Sam Walton helped her. Women would play an important role in Walton's rise as a major player in the retail industry.

Sam Walton, a military vet, met and married Helen Robson. Helen Robson was the daughter of L. S. Robson. L. S. Robson was a successful rancher and business owner. He organized his ranch and business as a partnership and made his children, including Helen, partners. Helen played an important role in her family's business. She had a degree in finance at a time when most women did not have advanced degrees. She kept the books for the family business. Sam later borrowed $20,000 from his father-in-law to purchase his first store. He adopted the model established by his father-in-law. He organized Wal-Mart, Inc. as a partnership, making his children partners. Madrick (2011) said Walton's early success was based on good economic times in the early 1970s and troubled economic times in the late 1970s.

Walton believed he could offer lower prices than his competitors and still offer high quality services to his customers. A recipient of the Presidential Medal of Freedom in 1992, Walton once said, "If we work together, we'll lower the cost of living for everyone . . . we'll give the world an opportunity to see what it's like to save and have a better life." Walton articulated ten rules for building a business, which he believed could be adopted by aspiring business owners. He outlined the rules in his book, *Sam Walton: Made in America*. Walton's first rule involved commitment. Business owners must be dedicated to their enterprise. Walton said he was able to overcome personal challenges by being passionate and loving his work. Loving what you do motivates business owners to do whatever it takes to be successful, claimed Walton.

Share the wealth is Walton's second rule for a successful business. Like his father-in-law, Walton articulated a belief in treating employees as partners. Employees should feel as though they have a personal stake in the company's future. "Offer discounted stock, and grant them stock for their retirement. It's the single best thing we ever did" (Walton 1992, p. 247). Although employees should be treated like partners, Walton said "Remain a corporation and retain control if you like, but behave as a servant leader" (Walton 1992, p. 247).

Walton's third rule for success in business was to motivate partners. It is not enough to offer economic incentives. Employees should be motivated and challenged everyday. Goal setting is key to success in business. Competition among employees is healthy and produces positive results. Embrace change, be flexible, "keep everybody guessing as to what your next trick is going to be" (Walton 1992, p. 247).

Communication is key, advised Walton. Partners should know as much as possible. Knowledge brings about greater understanding, concern, and loyalty, Walton believed. Walton warned, "If you don't trust your associates to know what's going on, they'll know you don't really consider them partners. Information is power, and the gain you get from empowering your associates more than offsets the risk of informing your competitors" (Walton 1992, p. 247).

For Walton there were different types of loyalty. There was the loyalty one garnered from distributing paychecks and stock options and then there was the loyalty earned when one feels appreciated. "Words of praise. They're absolutely free-and worth a fortune," wrote Walton (Walton 1992, p. 248).

In addition to commitment, motivation, sharing, communicating, and appreciation, Walton said successful business leaders celebrate success, listen, exceed customer expectations, maintain control, and do what everyone else is not doing. Walton said he learned that it was okay to fail and critically important to acknowledge success.

Engaging everyone in the company, according to Walton, was part of his success. For Walton it was important not only to listen to people in his company but also to encourage them to talk. "The folks on the front line—the ones who actually talk to the customer—are the only ones who really know what's going on out there. You'd better find out what they know. This really is what total quality is about. To push responsibility down in your organization, and to force good ideas to bubble up within it, you must listen to what your associates are trying to tell you" (Walton 1992, p. 248).

Successful businesses not only give customers what they want; successful businesses exceed expectations to keep customers coming back. Walton also advised business leaders to watch the "ratio of expenses to sales. You can make a lot of different mistakes and still recover if you run an efficient operation. Or you can be brilliant and still go out of business if you're too inefficient" (Walton 1992, p. 248–249). Finally, Walton advised businesses to "go the other way" (Walton 1992, pg. 249). Success may be found in the ability "to stay out in front" of change (Walton 1992, p. 249).

In the opening to his book, Walton (1992) wrote the following, "I realize that ours is a story about the kinds of traditional principles that made America great in the first place" (p. xiii). Walton (1992) added, "But I think more than anything it proves there's absolutely no limit to what plain, ordinary working people can accomplish if they're given the opportunity and the encouragement and the incentive to do their best" (p. xiii). Although, Walton conceded that his ten rules for success in business might appear to some as very simplistic, what is perhaps most revealing is the extent to which Walton's narrative and his rules point to a gap between how things should work in business, and in the broader society, and how business and the larger society actually work.

For example, while some business owners are passionate about what they do, some are far more passionate about what the business can do for them- namely increase their overall net worth. There is of course nothing wrong with anyone is a capitalist society wanting to make a profit, but the idea that people need to pursue their passions to be successful is simply not the case. The commitment lies not so much in the vocation, but in the pursuit of profit. Therefore, one can be dispassionate about their work and business, but passionate about the monetary benefits associated with it.

Although Walton expressed the importance of sharing profits with "all your associates," associates have historically not shared in the profits, especially in a way that "saves them money and live better lives." In fact, efforts on the part of associates or employees to unionize have time and time again been thwarted by Walton's company.

While Walton felt motivating employees was important and encouraged competition, the fact of the matter is that a number of Wal-Mart employees have documented unequal treatment, including when it came time to promote workers to management positions, which typically happens from within the corporation.

In a corporation with as many employees as Wal-Mart, Inc., it is hard to imagine how communication is filtered from the highest levels of the company to the lowest levels of the company and back again, as Walton suggested. Wal-Mart has long been viewed as the poster child of an American bureaucracy. Like virtually all other bureaucracies there are shortcomings. Despite Weber's contention that bureaucracies were highly rational organizations, characterized by great efficiency, it is widely accepted that bureaucracies are notoriously irrational and inefficient and create a host of problems throughout society. Large formal organizations, such as Wal-Mart often create feelings of alienation, so the idea that Wal-Mart or any other business, especially a business of Wal-Mart's size and influence, would and could communicate effectively, show appreciation, and listen to all those in its employ, is unlikely.

There is a great deal of research that challenges Walton's rules for success in business and his perspective on the effects of Wal-Mart, Inc. on the lives of individuals, families, neighborhoods, businesses, and the society as a whole. We now turn our attention to some of the research that focuses on what happens when and where Wal-Mart enters or expands.

WAL-MART: THE GOOD AND THE BAD?

Glandon and Jaremski (2014) examined how the presence of Wal-Mart impacts stores in surrounding communities. The researchers observed that Wal-Mart has fundamentally changed the retail landscape, especially since 1990 when the company grew from 300 stores in the United States to more than 4,400 locations, with one in every state. Wal-Mart's revenue is currently over eight percent of U.S. consumption expenditure on goods. About 80 percent of grocery stores identified Wal-Mart types stores were their biggest concern. When Wal-Mart's come to an area or expand in one where they already have footing, traditional retailers increased the frequency of their sales-periodic price reductions—to keep customers. However, Wal-Mart is consistently able to attract customers by setting their initial prices low and keeping them at those levels. Traditional leaders experience lost revenue, not due to a loss of customers but because of decreased baskets.

Ellickson and Grieco (2013) also examined the effects of Wal-Mart on retailing. The researchers found that in the case of grocery retailing the effects of Wal-Mart were geographically based. The firms most impacted by Wal-Mart were within a two-mile radius. Early on Wal-Mart's history the firms most impacted were small chains and small businesses. As Wal-Mart expanded into grocery retailing it is the larger chains that are most impacted. In grocery retailing there are high costs for travel and goods are perishable. Wal-Mart was able to shift the burden of transport from the company to consumers and create "economies of density" by tunneling previously diffuse demand to a central location. In essence, Wal-Mart changed urban and rural markets by focusing on fewer but bigger outlets. According to Ellickson and Grieco (2013), Wal-Mart was able to transform a reluctance to travel great distances for lower prices and more choices and Wal-Mart remains a major force in grocery retailing.

Logan (2013) challenges Wal-Mart's professed commitment to its workers in an article concerning "the mounting guerilla war against the reign of Wal-Mart." Workers have been dissatisfied with Wal-Mart for decades. Over the past twenty years, a segment of Wal-Mart's workforce has felt less like associates or partners, and more like the alienated workers Marx warned us about many years ago. Workers attempted to organize with limited success and were met with aggressive opposition. The Wake-Up Wal-Mart movement was initiated to raise awareness about working-conditions. The current focus, according to Logan (2013) is on activism as evidenced by a number of initiatives targeting Wal-Mart. The first strikes in the history of the company took place in the past few years and Logan (2013) predicts more strikes are likely.

Making Change at Wal-Mart outlined the negative effects of Wal-Mart on workers. Making Change at Wal-Mart is described as "a coalition of Wal-Mart associates, union members, small business owners, religious leaders, community organizations, woman's advocacy groups, multi-ethnic coalitions, elected officials and ordinary citizens who believe that changing Wal-Mart is vital for the future of our country." The group identifies a host of issues that run counter to the narrative laid out in Walton's book and in current literature from the company. For example, the group contends that Wal-Mart keeps employees in poverty by paying relatively low wages. The average wage is estimated at $8.81 according to the coalition's web site. Three local jobs are lost for every two jobs Wal-Mart creates in a community. Wal-Mart not only busted attempts for workers to unionize but created a "friendly environment" where workers would "accept" less pay (Madrick 2011). Additionally, while Wal-Mart employs a lot of people of color they often financially support candidates "who vote the wrong way on civil rights." Wal-Mart and the Walton Family Foundation has been linked to American Legislative Exchange Council (ALEC) which has supported what some characterize as voter suppression and stand your ground laws.

Adams (2013) published an article about an important ruling involving allegations of gender discrimination at Wal-Mart. Betty Dukes, a black woman, accused Wal-Mart of gender discrimination in 2001. She made the accusation that Wal-Mart paid women less and were more likely to promote males. What was significant about the case was the victory Dukes ultimately won in 2004. The U.S. District Court granted Dukes and female employees of Wal-Mart class certification, which created the potential for extending liability to other female workers. Given the size of Wal-Mart, the case was destined to be the largest class action suit ever in U.S. history at the time. However, in 2011 the U.S. Supreme Court reversed the ruling. Writing for the majority, Justice Scalia cited gender-neutral employment policies and the decentralized governance of Wal-Mart as reasons for the reversal. The court essentially questioned the "glue binding" the class together. The four conditions for class certification: numerosity, commonality, typicality, and adequacy of representation were not met, ruled the court.

According to Adams (2013), the ruling was viewed as a victory for big businesses like Wal-Mart and a defeat for workers and people of color. Wal-Mart was, after all, the nation's largest private, nongovernmental employer. The Duke case meant, "individual employees will have an increasingly difficult time in leveling the playing field in the David vs. Goliath battle over employee's rights and must be regarded as a victory for business (Adams 2013, p.265).

Research on the impact of Wal-Mart is focused not only on the impact of Wal-Mart on smaller businesses or on workers, but on the effect of social capital, religion, and even hate groups. Goetz and Rupasingha (2012) found a link between the presences of Wal-Mart and the numbers of hate groups. The researchers hypothesized that the presence of Wal-Mart contributed to alienation "by putting pressure on and driving small owner-operated retail establishments or through more subtle social impacts" (p. 383). Additionally, Wal-Mart stores tend to locate in places where hate groups form.

Wal-Mart stores may not contribute to a sense of community. Brunn (2006) examined advertising in an effort to assess the relationship between Wal-Mart and local communities. Wal-Mart tended to advertise on network television and on nationwide media. Although the aforementioned advertising strategy may be viewed as cost effective, it could also be viewed as insensitive to local communities and their individualized needs.

Wal-Mart also contributes to obesity and increased body mass indexes, according to research. Courtemanche (2011) found that an additional Wal-Mart Supercenter per one hundred thousand residents increased body mass index (BMI) by 0.24 units and the obesity rate by 2.3 percentage points. Wal-Mart Supercenters explain about ten percent of the rise in obesity in the late 1980s. The researchers think the lower food costs and higher opportunity costs associated with physical activity explained the outcomes. In other words, cheaper foods lead to great weight gain in some instances.

While Wal-Mart is recognized for its role in responding to disasters such as Hurricane Rita and Hurricane Katrina (Horwitz 2009), but there are also some concerns that Wal-Mart stores may have a negative effect on crime. Wolff and Pyrroz (2014) observed the impact of Wal-Mart on crime rates. As Wal-Mart was experiencing great growth in the 1990s, it was locating in areas where the crime rate was also quite high, but was Wal-Mart's entrance or expansion related to crime rates, wondered Wolff and Pyrroz (2014). Would the loss of small businesses lead to structural characteristics that might influence crime rates? The loss of business leaders might leave a void in community leadership that might limit the ability of the community to set and realize common goals and engage in efforts to regulate residents. The loss of small businesses might also cause residents to move away to find work and the influx of new residents might impact crime rates. Wolff and Pyrroz (2014) found that in counties with Wal-Mart stores the violent and property crime rates were higher. They also found that the presence of Wal-Mart stores does not necessarily increase or decrease crime.

Wal-Mart stores may, however, create political division and exacerbate racial and religious tensions due to the company's implicit and tacit appeal to evangelical Christians, based upon research by Rebekah Massengill (2011). While research has shown a consistent relationship between educational levels and attitudes about Wal-Mart, identifying as an evangelical trumps educational attainment. As educational levels increase favorable attitudes about Wal-Mart usually decrease. Education was not a significant determinant of attitudes toward Wal-Mart for evangelicals. The analysis of data collected by Pew Research may show that Wal-Mart's signaling to evangelical Christians is effective. Wal-Mart is known for carrying religious books and media aimed at evangelical Christians. Many evangelical Christians are located in the South where Wal-Mart has a lot of locations and residents have few other retail options. Massengill (2011) warned that the relatively favorable view of Wal-Mart and the frequency with which evangelicals flock to Wal-Mart may not represent a true choice. There may not be many alternatives to Wal-Mart in some communities, particularly in more rural areas. Pew Research found that about 57 percent of Southerners shopped at Wal-Mart regularly compared to 41 percent of people in the Midwest, 34 percent of people in the West, and 24 percent of people in the Northeast. Nevertheless, evangelicals tend to support what they view as Wal-Mart's commitment to "family, free enterprise and religious faith" (Massengill 2011, p. 70).

Wal-Mart not only effected the retail industry, including workers and the communities where they live, but Wal-Mart also effected how we think of ourselves as citizens, argued Collins (2011). Wal-Mart is responsible for shifting the very meaning of consumer citizenship in the United States, wrote Collins (2011). At the very heart of Keynesian ideology is the proper relationship between production and consumption and the appropriate area for civic engagement with the economy. Wal-Mart was instrumental in promoting the consumer over the citizen and the worker. Essentially, Wal-Mart replaced the "proper balance between production and consumption with a rhetoric of choice between low prices and high wages" (Collins 2011, 107).

The tension between the role of the state in the economy and the responsibilities of employers to workers did not begin (and will not end) with Wal-Mart. Collins (2011) traces these tensions to the early twentieth century to grassroots efforts to address the quality of food and drugs; to advocacy around antitrust laws; fair pricing; minimum wage; and fair labor practices. "Ethical consumption" and "union label" meant something then—with all their imperfections. The consumer citizen participated in efforts to strengthen the economy from rationing programs, increasing their savings, and serving as deputies over store prices.

The purchaser consumer and consumer citizen merged after the World War. Consumerism was viewed as one of the highest forms of patriotism, argued Collins (2011). By the 1970s Keynesianism declined in popularity (Krugman 2009) and the purchaser as citizen maintained popularity. Wal-Mart redefined consumer citizen with its focus on the car, one-stop shopping, and price as the most significant dimension of competition (Collins 2011).

Some business owners, especially larger business owners with wealth, status, and power, look at Sam Walton and Wal-Mart as a roadmap for success and think how can apply the Wal-Mart paradigm to some area of the global economy and enjoy similar success. Over the past view decades it is becoming increasingly clear that many of these business owners have set their sites on public education as the next big thing, following the pathway of Sam Walton. The most significant lessons these business owners have learned from Walton are not in the ten rules for a successful business that Walton (1992) wrote about his memoir, but in the Walton Family's and Wal-Mart, Inc.'s hidden curriculum.

HIDDEN CURRICULUM

Sam Walton was able to grow a business in the best and in the worst economic times. This is due in large part to the finding that when hard economic times hit the United States some groups are hurt more than others. In some ways the wealthiest Americans are less vulnerable to market changes because unlike average Americans they seldom have all of their eggs in one basket. The wealthiest Americans have diversified portfolios, which prevent them from losing most, if not all, of their overall net worth during an economic downturn, such as in the case of a recession. Tom Clark addressed these and other issues in his book with Anthony Heath (Clark and Heath 2014). The book, *Hard Times: The Divisive Toll of the Economic Slump* was the subject of an in-depth interview published online by *Salon*.

Reflecting on the effect of the Great Recession on America and the United Kingdom, the following assertion is made, "While the stock market can always bounce back and corporate profits can always recover, for millions of people who lost opportunities to build financial stability for themselves from which to help create a healthy, broader community, the social ills born from the Great Recession will last a life time." Clearly people experience economic downturns differently based upon their socioeconomic status at the onset of crisis. In fact, the point is made that those that are insulated the most by their walls of wealth and fortresses of fortune often "divert attention away from their destructive economic policies and shift the blame instead onto the so-called 47-percent, the very people most harmed by the Great Recession." There is evidence of this in the educational reform movement, particularly in the movement to privatize public schools, and in the illusion of school choice. Investment into the privatization of public education is not contingent upon variations in the resources available to schools. In other words profits are not necessarily greater when resources for public schools are lower or lower when resources for public schools are higher; rather, opportunities to generate profits exists, but may be packaged differently based upon economic conditions.

There is never a bad time to benefit could be the motto for elites. Walton was able to capitalize on the disadvantaged and marginality of a group and appear as if he was doing something altruistic. Not only did Walton benefit from the misery of low-income folks in rural areas who were largely ignored or forgotten by mainstream society, but also he realized that the individuals in the areas where his economic dynasty began were just the tips of the iceberg. There were marginalized and disadvantaged people throughout the country and he set-up shop in many of those places. Disadvantaged individuals were not only in rural and urban areas in the U.S., but they could be found throughout the globe. Preaching an economic gospel of savings and the good life appealed to many individuals who longed for the opportunity to do just that, save and live a better life. Similarly, so-called capitalist educational reforms recognize that there are marginalized and disadvantaged people throughout the country whose children are in under resourced schools that are not adequately preparing them for success in schools and beyond. They recognize that the public school system is not in a state of crisis; rather, the public school system is continuing to function as it was designed-to privilege some and disadvantage others-and they need only preach an educational gospel of academic success and promises of a better life and they too with reap Walton-like benefits and have the support of local communities, including elected officials, and even parents. When times are good capitalist educational reformers pull students into their schools with promises that they will prepare them for the jobs of the future and in harsh economic times capitalist educational reformers emphasize the "free" public education open to students, masking the real cost to the child, family, community, and society when helping the few, hurts the many.

Walton also taught capitalist educational reformers the significance of eliminating true choice. Why are some individuals, particularly in the South, so loyal to Wal-Mart? What keeps them coming back for groceries and other goods? Does Wal-Mart provide superior products? Does Wal-Mart provide a shopping experience that you simply can't get anywhere else? In many places where Wal-Mart's are located there is no true choice. Alternatives have virtually been eliminated. When and where Wal-Mart enters, or expands, smaller businesses disappear or must change how they do business in order to compete. Businesses may have to reinvent themselves and provide some type of specialized service to retain customers or to attract new customers. Business that may have sold an array of merchandise in the past may opt to sell one particular item or find their niche in some other ways. Limiting the types of products sold may make patronizing the local business irrational for someone with limited financial resources and limited access to personal transportation. Additionally, the number of businesses in search of no, or low, skilled workers in areas in close proximity to individuals with no or low skills are few and far between. Wal-Mart offers employment opportunities in small towns and communities where major industries once thrived, and/or where smaller industries dominated, but later abandoned. Wal-Mart locations also offer flexible shifts with many locations open 24-hours, 7-days a week. With limited employment options due to spatial mismatches and other structural issues, what true choices might individuals in the communities described here really have?

Capitalist economic reformers, with the tacit support of elected officials and other public policymakers, eliminate true choice, all the while espousing the virtues of school choice. In far too many public school districts more than one school is designated as failing based upon measures determined by individuals and organizations external to local schools. Some of the decision-makers may even benefit monetary, or in other ways, from the outcomes. What real choice do parents and local school districts have when a poor letter grade is assigned to a neighborhood school? Can a parent in good conscious continue to send their child to a stigmatized school that now wears what is akin to the scarlet letter of the American public school system? Pop-up schools like magnet schools, charter schools, private schools, even gifted and talented programs, emerge and suddenly parents are told they have options; suddenly, parents have choices. Parents may continue to send their children to aged and failing schools where teachers and students are blamed for causing and contributing to their circumstances, or they may choose to send their children to a school, often in a brand new building with state-of-the-art equipment with promises of a better life. Educational reformists eliminate true choice by their very existence and the clever manner in which they market themselves using social media and indigenous social institutions. Contemporary educational reformers use the official language of the so-called post-racial era. The official language of the post-racial era includes articulating the values and principles of a fair and justice society without acting in a way that is reflective of either fairness or justice.

The U.S. Supreme Court may have saved Wal-Mart, Inc., millions of dollars in damages by refusing to recognize female workers as a class. The finding that much of Wal-Mart's workforce was decentralized, and that policies and procedures were gender neutral, was the saving grace. Although economic benefits, responsibility, and accountability usually flow from the top down in formal organizations like Wal-Mart, the fact that there were so many Wal-Mart stores with many layers of management, decision-making authority, and so forth that worked to the company's benefit. The same company that claims its employee as associates, which denotes some form of connectedness or relationship, was quick to point out the decentralization of power.

While most Americans live within fifteen miles of a Wal-Mart store many would be hard pressed to locate a single advertisement geared specifically for their local community. Although Wal-Mart might provide community support for certain groups, such as evangelical Christians, in the materials they sell and refuse to sell, there is little evidence that Wal-Mart advertises with specific local communities in mind. In its advertising Wal-Mart includes, like other global corporations, generic messages for consumers. Wal-Mart's approach to advertising is an efficient and cost effective approach to advertising, but amounts to a one-size fits all approach to marketing and a lack of understanding and appreciation for the uniqueness of local towns and communities. Wal-Mart's goal is allegedly to help people save money and live better and advertisements routinely feature parents and children saving money in Wal-Mart and making purchases that help their individual families, even local schools. It is not clear that Wal-Mart as an organization is committed to such values. Nonetheless, saving money and living better are the words Wal-Mart claims to live by. The message: Wal-Mart cares about its customers saving money and living a better quality of life and other companies only care about themselves.

Individuals interested in benefiting from the misery heaped upon students, parents, and teachers in under resourced schools have apparently learned a lot from Wal-Mart's messaging. Entities such as KIPP and Imagine Schools and even Cristo Rey, advertise to a broad audience. These "networks" advertise to the most disadvantaged, with the hopes of selling an ideal and a set of values. Never mind that their very presence may have a negative impact on public schools, or the idea that while they may help some and harm many, for-profit and pseudo public schools hone in on the very American values that have alluded people of color for most of the nation's history.

One need only conduct a content analysis of the official websites for each entity to see which values the companies believe will capture the interest of marginalized and disadvantaged parents, such that they will essentially turn their backs on the majority of children in their communities for the off-chance that their child may be one of the few "saved" from the sinking ship that is American public education, especially in urban and rural communities.

KIPP is a public charter school founded in 1994. On the official web page KIPP describes itself as a national network of "free" "public schools." In bold letters the following appears, "Work hard. Be nice." Images of students and teachers of color abound. KIPP identifies it target audience as "educationally underserved communities." KIPP vows to assist students in developing "knowledge, skills, character and habits" needed for success at the post-secondary level and globally. KIPP claims to hope to see a day when "all public schools will help children develop the knowledge, skills, character, and habits necessary to achieve their dreams while making the world a better place."

The purposeful choice of words must not be overlooked. KIPP is careful to mention that the schools are free. Most alternatives to traditional public schools usually involve some form of tuition. KIPP wants parents and prospective communities to know—or at least believe—that there is no cost to parents and therefore no risk. Students who attend what KIPP describes as educationally underserved communities are often times also economically disadvantaged. So the financial cost of a KIPP education is within budget.

KIPP wants parents to feel that their schools are safe because students are nice and because the school focuses on character building. The issue of school safety is one that parents from educationally underserved and economically disadvantaged schools contend with. KIPP is trying to communicate to parents and students that not only will their children learn the skills they need for success in life, but it is free and safe. KIPP's message also reinforces stereotypes that the public schools students in their targeted demographic attend are not only failing to teach students and thus not preparing them for college or the world of work, but that they also are filled with students who lack character, may be violent, and are therefore unsafe.

Imagine Schools has a very similar approach to advertising their schools, but feature images of students from across the racial and ethnic spectrum and the one teacher featured was a white female. Imagine Schools describe their approach as "value-based." The values include "justice" "integrity" and "fun." Imagine Schools claim to produce "leaders" and focus on success as defined as academic growth, character development, parent choice, economic sustainability, and school development.

Imagine Schools is clearly trying to capitalize on the dream of an integrated school environment in keeping with the type of world King and other dreamed about or imagined. Students and parents in economically disadvantaged schools and communities are not strangers to injustice, imaging a school where justice is a focal appoint is appealing as is a learning environment where integrity and fun are valued. Testing and other scandals have long since called into question the integrity of some public schools and what some teachers and parents consider too great an emphasis on testing, returning fun to the learning environment is appealing. As was the case with KIPP, Imagine Schools promise to produce students who live "honorable lives." Imagine Schools markets itself as everything traditional public schools are not and say little about the challenges it, or similar institutions face and have faced throughout the years.

Cristo Rey is a national network of schools aimed at "underrepresented urban youth" but differs from KIPP and Imagine Schools principally because it is also a Catholic institution. Cristo Rey also promises to prepare students for success in college and life and plans to accomplish the goal "through rigorous academics, coupled with real world work experience." Cristo Rey incorporated in 2003 and operated schools in Los Angeles, Portland, and Denver, according to the office web site for the organization. Investments from the Bill and Melinda Gates Foundation in 2003 provided seed money for the organization and with more than $1.6 million from The Walton Family Foundation "to accelerate growth, primarily in states that have either vouchers or tax-credits." To be part of the "network" schools "serves only economically disadvantaged students" of all religious, racial and ethnic backgrounds. Schools must also be family centered and play an active role in the local community. Students must participate in work-study, and support graduates throughout their college career. Unlike KIPP and Imagine Schools, Cristo Rey is quite explicit about its business roots. Jesuit Father John Foley was convinced of the need for an "unconventional approach to education" and that approach included a plan "to implement an innovative business model whereby students work five days each month in an entry-level job at a professional company, with the fee for their work being directed to underwrite tuition costs." While the phrase "character development" does not appear in the "mission effectiveness standards" it is clearly implied in the schools motto. Cristo Rey of the three the most forthcoming about its funding source and its adaptation of business models to public education. Cristo Rey appeals to parents who want of the trimmings of a parochial education that has far beyond their reach. It is not clear how Cristo Rey's requirement of students to work to offset the cost of tuition is any different than suggestions by people like former Speaker of the House Newt Gingrich that poor children should work in the schools that they attend to teach them a sense of work ethic.

Within the Wal-Mart hidden curriculum are the topics of self-regulation and collective efficacy of local communities. By bypassing local media and using its considerable dollars for national outlets, Wal-Mart further whittles away the social cohesion and social capital of communities where residents are among the most disadvantaged in the nation and throughout the world. There is already evidence that the presence of Wal-Mart can lead to a loss of small businesses and local leaders. There is also evidence that the loss of such businesses fosters social disorganization and can contribute to crimes against people and property. The potential loss of leadership and the weakening of social ties make efforts to resist the downside of the effects of Wal-Mart and other issues plaguing urban and rural communities, which benefits

Wal-Mart and others in positions of privilege who would not like to see historically disadvantaged groups mobilized, organized, and willing to power and revitalize.

Educational reformers are demonstrating proficiency in suppressing the self-regulation and collective efficacy of local communities. Some are even succeeding in redefining schools as the anchor institutions in historically disadvantaged communities and the center of the village. Pop-up schools and other so-called school choice options have contributed to the closure of schools throughout the United States, but especially in districts that are majority minority, such as in Chicago. Schools have historically served as places where social interaction takes place. Schools have historically played an important role in creating a sense of community—of connectedness. In the past and in many more affluent and more privileged communities, the teachers and administrators came out of the communities in which they taught, or at the very least could identify with the historic struggle of the students they taught. In more contemporary times, children of color are increasingly more likely to be educated in pseudo-public schools with staff members who do not look like them or who do not identify with the historical struggle of people in America and whom may see students of color as problems rather than pupils.

Additionally, since the new school choice movement, far too many schools have conceptualized the school as the epicenter of communal life, not as in integral part of it. Public schools in the modern age, particularly those targeting economically disadvantaged children and/or children of color see two other significant anchor institutions as part of the problem and not the solution. Families and churches have been demoted in their level of importance in the school choice age. Families are deemed important, but the focus is often on modifying the behavior of parents to meet the expectations of the school and not the school meeting the expectations and the needs of families. While some clergy may receive invitations to serve in advisory positions or serve as a conduit for recruiting students, there is little evidence that the black church plays a central role in these schools as they have historically in American public schools.

Another important lesson in the Wal-Mart hidden curriculum is the benefit of creating an illusion of a culture of cooperation. While the house that Sam Walton built was hit by discord and allegations of inequality, Walton and his successors have created an institutional culture where consumers and many workers feel part of something bigger than themselves. The Walton's consistently articulate a commitment to families, faith, and to the nation despite allegations to the contrary. The idea that individuals with relatively low incomes would be greeted as they walked into a retail store and not treated immediately with distain or outright ignored, which is far too often the case for historically disadvantaged individuals. Workers would not be referred to as mere employees, but as associates and partners, while clearly not sharing the wealth.

Pop-up schools have followed Walton's lead and also work toward creating a culture of cooperation. The leaders of the "national networks" may call upon people in the local area to assist with the establishment of schools and the identification of potential locations, but their roles are more likely to reflect tokenism than more meaningful forms of participation. Arnstein's (1969) classic model of public participation is useful here in understanding the ceremonial role that local leaders may play in the new reform movement. Arnstein (1969) described real participation, which was characterized by decision-making authority and institutional power. Manipulation and therapy are two other forms of participation where individuals have no authority or power "but simply represent a way to vent frustration" (Green and Haines 2012, p. 65).

Wal-Mart attracts a lot of applicants due in part to its proximity to historically disadvantaged communities where educational opportunities are often scarce or non-existent, and the limited educational requirements is appealing to individuals from what KIPP calls "educationally underserved communities." Wal-Mart employs people with less than a high school diploma or GED. Experience is not a prerequisite for employment at Wal-Mart for hourly and part-time positions. Similarly, experience in education is not a prerequisite for managing a school or educational policy. One need only look at the professional backgrounds of the chief officers of some of the national charter schools identified in this book and even among some board members and school administrators.

Jason Bryant, CEO and President of Imagine Schools was responsible for "operation oversight" of power plants in California before joining Imagine Schools in 2005. Isabel Berio, Senior Vice President was a litigation attorney in Chicago and previous worked as a fundraiser. Barry Sharp, CEO and President of Imagine Schools Non-Profit was the Chief Financial Officer at AES, the power plan company where Bryant also worked, where held the distinction of being the third longest serving Chief Financial Officer in a Fortune 500 firm. When it comes to reforming public schools in America, some have learned that no experience is necessary.

The final lesson in Sam Walton's hidden curriculum is to include and exclude unapologetically. The location of Wal-Mart stores in rural and urban areas impacted the surrounding communities, admittedly with varying results. The communities that were included into the Wal-Mart family of stores at least had the potential to increase the economic development of the area and to provide struggling workers with the opportunity to work again. At the same time, areas where Sam Walton and his successors did not open locations remained in isolation. Walton could not "save" everyone, so he had to come to embrace the fact that including some meant excluding others. In other words, some consumers, workers and communities had the opportunity to benefit from Wal-Mart's presence.

Capitalist educational reformers are good students and have learned to be comfortable with include some and excluding others. Charter, and other units of school choice, fully understand that they do not have the capacity to "save" every child in an underperforming, under resourced, or unsafe school, but also recognize by attempting or claiming to assist a few can still generate profits, even with the understanding that far more students will continue to be ill-prepared for the jobs or today and tomorrow. Capitalist educational reformers do not see education as a civil right, but as a revenue generator. American public schools represent fertile grounds where elites can use their superior wealth, power, and influence, to create a niche in the public school educational reform industry and move more of the largest remaining sectors of the public center into the control of the private sector.

The most important lessons cannot be found in Walton's rules for a successful business, nor can the most important lessons come from merely analyzing the company's and the family's influence in the educational reform movement. The most important lessons are found in Walton's hidden curriculum, which provides a blueprint for capitalists to operate in the so-called colorblind or post-racial era. In this chapter I examined the history of Wal-Mart stores. I reviewed the biography of Wal-Mart's founder, Sam Walton, and the ten rules for success in business. I explored the many lessons contemporary educational reformers learned from Walton's hidden curriculum. I identified ways in which the Walton model is being applied to efforts to privatize public education or at least enrich the bottom line of entrepreneurs. In the next chapter I explore the impact of the changing purpose of education in the lives of a forgotten segment of the population: the black working-class.

Chapter Five

Education and Today's Black Working-Class: Low Quality, Low Prices, Low Wages

The black working-class has played an important role in the history of this nation from their pivotal role in the Civil Rights Movement to their everyday contributions to the U.S. economy as producers and consumers. The current educational reform movement is destined to have a deleterious impact on Americans regardless of race and class, but will hit members of the black working-class particularly hard. I argue that the black working-class is already showing signs of the effects of the Wal-Martization of public education, especially in the post-Civil Rights Movement where public policies in general, and educational policies in particular, tend to target and benefit the middle-class, or address the poor, and virtually ignore the black working-class.

In the case of public education reform there are a number of reasons why the black working-class is hardest hit. The working-class is the modal category for blacks in America. In other words, black have historically been more likely to be working-class than middle-class or poor. Working-class blacks will have limited access to neighborhoods where public schools are adequately resourced due to their race and/or class. Working-class blacks will also not have the resources to send their children to private schools because tuitions are too high, even with partial scholarships. Finally, given the commitment to social justice issues among working-class blacks, I argue that the black working-class are among the least likely to abandon the public school system and are best positioned to bring about positive changes. In other words, the black working-class has the least number of safety nets of any racialized social class. In this chapter I examine the size of the black working-class. I also examine the role that the black working-class has played in American society over time. I explore how disadvantaged the black working-class is relative to whites in the working-class. I make the case that current educational reform trends will clog up the pipeline from working-class-to-middle-class status for blacks and may also remove safety nets for those that slip into the bottom-class.

SIZE MATTERS: THE BLACK WORKING-CLASS

Social class is not an easy concept to grasp or measure. Social scientists disagree about how to best measure social class. Krieger et al. (1997) provided a review of how public health scholars have addressed the issue of measuring social class given the significance of income and wealth inequality in determining a host of public health outcomes. Krieger et al. (1997) define social class "to refer to social groups arising from interdependent economic relationships among people" (p. 345). Social classes "exist in relationship to and co-define each other" (p. 345). Social class may be measured at many levels, including at the individual, household, or neighborhood level, wrote the authors, and across time and place. Krieger et al. (1997) draws from the work of sociologist Erik Olin Wright (1985) to highlighting measurements of social class where social classes can best be understood "in complex intersections of three forms of exploitation involving: (a) ownership of capital assets, (b) control of organization assets, and (c) possession of skill or credential assets" (Krieger et al. 1997, p. 350). Four classes emerge from the aforementioned view of social class: wage laborers; petty bourgeois; small employers; and capitalists.

While Wright (1985) explained social classes as a series of social relations, others explain social classes almost exclusively as occupational, argued Krieger et al. (1997). Widely used in Europe, social class is measured by one's standing within the community which results in the emergence of five categories of class: professional, intermediate, skilled non-manual, skilled manual, partly skilled, and unskilled (Krieger et al. 1997). In short, occupational prestige determines social class position. According to Krieger et al. (1997), "one limitation of socioeconomic indicators based on occupational classifications is that they may not comparably capture disparities in working and living conditions across divisions of race/ethnicity and gender" and occupationally-based categories of social class "cannot readily be used for social groups outside of the recognized paid labor. These groups include: non-retired adults who are unemployed, homemakers (chiefly women) who do not work outside of the home, persons employed in informal or illegal sectors of the economy, and also groups not expected to be in the active labor force, i.e., children and retired adults" (Krieger et al. 1997, p. 351).

Beyond the issues of social relationships, Krieger et al. (1997) also reviewed measures of income, poverty, wealth, education, deprivation, and prestige. Income may be used to measure social class, but income can be difficult to measure with all of its varying components and at all levels of the social world. Similarly, poverty may be used to measure social classes in relation to income given that there are official guidelines established by the United States government, for example, to measure poverty.

Krieger et al. (1997) addressed the matters of material and social deprivations in their review of how to best measure social class. Material deprivation addresses housing needs, access to food, and so forth, whereas social deprivation addresses access to employment and key social institutions. Social classes may be determined using not only measures of income, poverty, and deprivation but of overall net worth and privilege. Among the most widely used measures of social class in public health research is education (Krieger et al. 1997).

Education is by far easier to measure than income, poverty, social deprivation, wealth, and privilege and is used most often in public health research, but there are some concerns with relying on education alone as a measure of social class. Although educational attainment is a stable measurement, using it "may preclude capturing how changes in economic well-being in adulthood can alter health status" for example (Krieger et al. 1997, p. 364). Moreover, the concept of education is a social construct and its meaning can vary across place and time. Furthermore, returns on investments into education vary for individuals with membership in historically disadvantaged groups.

Social scientists have attempted to capture social class by taking into consideration more than one of the measurements discussed here. The creation of indices to measure social class is common in the literature. Otis Duncan's Socioeconomic Index (SEI) is a classic example. Duncan used income, education, and occupational prestige. Others have used "the Nam-Powers Occupational Status Score, based on the median income and education of persons employed in a given occupation: and the Nam-Powers Socioeconomic Status Score, which combines the Nam-Powers Occupational Status Score for a given individual's occupation with the person's educational level and family income. A fourth measure, the Hollingshead Index of Social Position, combines information on an individual's educational level and occupational rank" (Krieger et al. 1997, p. 366).

Diemer et al. (2012) described how social class is measured in psychological research and there are some similarities and differences. Diemer et al. (2012) use a sociological definition of social class and define it as "the higher order construct representing an individual or group's relative position in an economic-social-cultural hierarchy. We define social class as denoting power, prestige, and control over resources" (Diemer et al. 2002, p. 72). For psychologists measuring social class has historically meant using an index constructed on one's access to income, wealth, education, and occupational prestige or a subjective measure which involves "one's perception of his or her social class" (Diemer et al. 2002, p. 79).

Sociologists, such as Otis Duncan, played key roles in developing ways to measure social class and continue to do so with innovative ways of thinking about social class at all levels of society. Sociologists have linked social class with a host of outcomes such as teaching in bilingual settings (Shine and Otheguy 2013); religion (Schwadel 2012); structured activity participation for children (Bennett, Lutz, and Jayaram 2012); health (Layte & Whelan 2009; Springer and Mouzon 2011; Walsh, Torr, and Bui 2010); and racial socialization (Crouter et al. 2008). The ways in which social class is measured is often as varied as the subject matters to which social class are linked. A review of recent articles published in the journals, *American Sociological Review* and *Sociology of Education,* are good examples.

Bennett, Lutz, and Jayaram (2012) used education to measure social class. Drawing from the works of classical sociologists such as Max Weber (1947), the researchers discussed education as a determinant of other measures of overall economic well-being including income and occupational prestige. They addressed social class as both culture and structural location in their analyses of two middle school in the northeast. Middle-class families had at least one spouse with a bachelor's degree and all other families were considered working-class. About 60 percent of the working-class families earned less than $25,000 a year compared to 60 percent of middle-class families who earned more than $75,000 per year. The researchers found that structural location explained more of the variations in structured activity participation than culture. In addition to the small sample size and generalizability to the study findings, another important limitation is the authors' decision not to distinguish between working-class and poor families who may have very different access to resources that may impact the quality and quality of structured activity participation for their children.

Condron (2009) published a study about racial differences in children's learning in the flagship journal for sociology, *American Sociological Review.* Condron (2009) examines the effects of social class on children's learning in a relatively unconventional way. As noted in the 2009 article, "socioeconomic status is confounded with other non-school factors explaining the black/white achievement gap." Condron's (2009) approach was to view social class as "a key analytic category that contributes to inequality in school years through both its distinct non-school mechanisms and its association with race." Condron (2009) distinguished between working-class and poor families. Children were considered "working-class if both parents have less than a bachelor's degree and did not work in an executive, administrative, or managerial position and their household income is above the poverty line." Poor families had household incomes below the poverty line regardless of the educational attainment or occupation of the parents. Condron's (2009) study found that schools make black/white inequalities worse while slowing growth of social classes in the analysis on first graders. Achievement gaps grow during the school year, while the class gap widens during the summer months.

Both of the studies from the journal of *Sociology of Education* and *American Sociological Review* have some limitations, but the studies represent a focus on the working-class that has been relatively understudied over the past several decades. Most sociologists have not responded to a call issued by a group of sociologists in the millennial issue of *American Sociological Review*.

Horton et al. (2000) were concerned about the volume of published articles on race and social class, which focused on either the black middle-class, or on poor blacks. The publication of William Julius Wilson's book, *The Declining Significance of Race,* had a tremendous impact on the sociological literature on race and social class. In the classic work, Wilson made the argument that race was no longer the determining factor in the lives of people of African descent in America. Whereas, blacks experienced unequal treatment because of the racial group to which they were assigned in the past, things changed. Wilson made the argument that structural economic changes as well as legislative changes associated with the modern day civil rights movement forever changed the experiences of people of color in the United States, to one that was determined by race to one that was more heavily influenced by social class. The experiences of blacks in the middle-class were no longer in sync with blacks with membership in lower-classes.

By Wilson's count, the arguments laid out his book appear in almost a thousand empirical studies. Wilson revisited his classic work in a 2011 article published in *American Academy of Arts & Sciences* where he seeks to clarify the misconceptions regarding his views on race and class that created such a furor in the sociology and beyond. Wilson's made premise was that "changes in the system of production and in government have affected, over time, black/white access to rewards and privileges as well as racial antagonism" (p. 55). Wilson's original objectives were two-fold: "to explain historical developments in U.S. race relations and to account for paradoxical changes in the black class structure whereby, beginning in the last few decades of the twentieth century, the social and economic conditions of the black poor deteriorated while those of the black middle-class improved" (p. 55–56).

Wilson recalled his focus on three important moments in American history: "the preindustrial period of antebellum slavery and the early postbeullum era; the industrial period that began in the last quarter of the nineteenth century and ended at roughly the New Deal era; and the modern industrial post-World War II era" (p. 56). Racial oppression, argued Wilson, "was characteristic of both the preindustrial and industrial periods of American race relations" (p. 56). Wilson further made the argument that along with the different forms of racial oppression, the transition from a preindustrial to an industrial system led to a rise in the economic and political resources of black people in the United States and the increase in the number of industrial jobs served as one of the important pull factors attracting blacks from the South to the North and West in what became known as the Great Migration. In the years that followed World War II, Wilson said, "black class structure began to take on some characteristics of white class structure and that economic class gradually became more important than race in determining the life chances of individual African Americans" (p. 56). Despite claims to the contrary Wilson (2011) maintained, "was not that race is longer significant or that racial barriers between blacks and whites have been eliminated. Rather, in comparing the contemporary situation of African Americans to their situation in the past, the diverging experiences of blacks along class lines indicate that race is no longer the primary determinant of life chances for blacks (in the way it had been historically" (p. 56).

Others have written about the declining significance of race, including Eugene Robinson, Pulitzer Prize winning author and regular contributor to *MSNBC,* recently published a book where he described the declining significance of race. Although Robinson did not make the linkages between structural changes and racial antagonism that Wilson made, but based on his observations of class differences within the black population declared the disintegration of black America into four groups: the transcendent elite, the mainstream middle, the abandoned, and the emergent.

The transcendent elite includes upper middle-class blacks that also occupy positions of influence and power. Black athletes in high-revenue generating sports, select black entertainers, black political leaders, and so forth, are members of the black transcendent elite. The social and economic standing of the transcendent elite is such that people of all racial and ethnic groups pause and take note of them.

THE BLACK WORKING-CLASS AND SOCIAL JUSTICE

The failure to adequately address what is happening to the black working-class in America and how changes to public education over the past several decades exacerbates many issues is especially critical given the role the black working-class has historically played in first for the rights of not only people of the African Diaspora, but other historically disadvantaged groups and the broader society. The black working-class has played a historic role in the labor and civil rights movements as examples.

The commitment of the black working-class to social justice issues may be found throughout history. Despite the controversies surrounding how to define the working-class it can be shown that workers who are not living in poverty and have not historically had the benefit of employment in professional occupations, or in occupations where they can yield both power and influence over others, and have not had the luxury of earning a bachelor's degree, represent the working-class in America. Given the racial discrimination blacks historically faced in this country and the discrimination they continue to face today, it is not hard to imagine the relative size of the group or its impact on virtually every social institution and social movement. Particularly in the period following the reconstruction era when blacks were able to compete against whites and others in the labor market, albeit with vast limitations, we see the black working-class not only emerge but emerge as a force to be reckoned with at all levels of society. It was the black working-class that was perhaps most empowered by the successes of mavericks like Jack Johnson, the first black heavyweight-boxing champion of the world. In the early part of the twentieth century boxing was considered a sport enjoyed by working-class Americans and viewed as a low-culture sport by many blacks and whites in the middle-class and among elites.

Jack Johnson was not only a prolific boxer, but with every victory against a white opponent he struck a blow against the dominant racialized ideology, which claimed white supremacy and black inferiority. It was the disadvantaged black working-class that were most captivated by what Johnson accomplished and it was the sense of power and empowerment he provided black working-class people with that was viewed as such a threat that laws were passed banning fight films. It was not a coincidence that Johnson's victories set-off race riots throughout the country and even led to the lynching of black men. The threat Johnson and his legion of black working-class supporters posed to the status quo also led to the passage of the Mann Act and Johnson's unjust conviction of violating it. The dominant racial group in America could not find ways to defeat Johnson and the sense of pride his victories instilled in the black working-class in the ring, so as Stanley Crouch put it, the dominant racial group in America did what they did when the South lost the war, they sent the law after Johnson.

Another important example of the black working-class and its commitment to social justice issues can be found in the work of Pullman car porters, organized and led by A. Phillip Randolph. Horton and I also addressed the historic role of Randolph as a labor leader for the black working-class and his strategic use of the press.

Asa Phillip Randolph used the publication *The Messenger* to assist in organizing and mobilizing black labor. In the issues of the publication, Randolph was able to showcase what he and others viewed as the failures of capitalism (Moreno 2006). Randolph, who co-founded the magazine, which had readers all across the United States, called black and white workers to work towards political and economic advancement. Randolph viewed socialism as the best economic and political system for riding the United States of its unequal treatment of workers, but black workers in particular.

Randolph's views about the need to eliminate racism and embrace socialism were well known. He tried to get black and white workers to see that they had much more in common than they had differences. Black and white workers both suffered under capitalism and shared an interest in working toward better wages, shorter work days, and improved working conditions. Randolph believed there was power in numbers. Working in concert black and white workers would have more leverage and compel those in positions of authority to acquiesce to their common demands. For Randolph, all the victories the working-class enjoyed were hard-fought and were won because "the employing class recognize no race lines. They will exploit a white man as readily as a black man. They will exploit women as readily as men. They will even go to the extent of coining the labor, blood and suffering of children into dollars. The introduction of women and children into the factories proves that capitalists are only concerned with profits and that they will exploit any race or class in order to make profits, whether they be black or white men, black or white women or black or white children."

While Randolph thought class was of critical importance, he did not ignore race. However, like others Asa Phillip Randolph saw racial conflict as a byproduct of class conflict. Randolph made the argument that blacks were used because of profit interests, not race. What some white workers saw as racial antagonism, Randolph described as actions any worker would take regardless of race. Randolph clearly wanted to appeal to the shared experiences of being a worker and not the differences associated with having membership in different racial groups. This was most evident in the following statement from Randolph, "it is idle and vain to hope or expect Negro workers, out of work and who receive less wages at work than white workers, to refuse scab upon white workers when an opportunity presents itself." Black and white workers had to "show that labor, black and white, is conscious of its interests and power. This will prove that unions are not based on race lines, but upon class lines. This will serve to convert a class or workers, which has been used by the capitalist to defeat organized labor, into an ardent, class conscious, intelligent, militant group."

Randolph also worked to show how intimately connected the media and elites were to one another. He described some of the major papers of the day as "the mouth piece of the present administration," but also "a plutocratic mouth piece." Randolph was marked by these publications and by many elites as a radical and an agitator.

Randolph's critique of capitalism was not widely embraced by many of the workers he tried to organize and mobilize or by many other black leaders of the day. The black and white working-class were loyal to capitalism as were other Americans. willingness to embrace socialism in a society deeply entrenched in capitalism led many to distance themselves from Randolph. Randolph was outwardly critical of black leaders, such as Booker T. Washington. Speaking on Washington, Randolph once said, "Booker Washington and all of them have simply advocated the Negroes get more work. The editors of *The Messenger* are not interested in Negroes getting more work. Negroes have too much work already. What we want Negroes to get is less work and more wages, with more leisure for study and recreation."

Randolph's commitment to social justice was symbolic of the commitment to social justice that many blacks in the working-class demonstrated during the twentieth century and like other civically engaged members of the black working-class, found his work and his publication under the watchful eye of elites and government. He also encouraged blacks facing violent racial mobs to defend themselves. Randolph's news magazine was considered one of the most dangerous in the nation. Randolph and the cofounder of *The Messenger* were arrested in "for treason, and the Postmaster General of the United States revoked the magazine's bulk rate postage status, which was not reinstated" (Jimoh 2005, p. 1081–1082).

Randolph became less radical over time and eventually became the first president of the Brotherhood of Sleeping Car Porters (BSCP). By the mid-1920s, *The Messenger*, was the official magazine of BSPC at which time the editors shared union news and views. "The magazine's founders managed to make it a venue for important cultural and intellectual exchanges that early on refused to replicate for its primarily Black leadership both the dominate discourse among New Negro intellectuals as well as the dominating discourse in the country" (Jimoh 2005, p. 1084).

Although members of the black working-class played important roles in efforts to create a more just and a more equitable society, the black working-class has been largely lost in the storm of contemporary research on race and class especially research about the Civil Rights Movement and the post-Civil Rights era. The dominant narratives surrounding a number of social justice issues exclude the role of the black working-class. This is true of the modern day Civil Rights Movement and the labor movement. Asimakopoulos (2010) work where the researcher challenged conventional wisdom about the Civil Rights Movement and the Black Power Movement as a largely black middle-class struggle. Asimakopoulos (2010) highlighted the efforts of the black working-class in the fight against the oppression they faced and continue to face. The black working-class was able to engage in the fight despite efforts to suppressed what was viewed as a real threat to capitalist and government.

Zeitlin and Weyher (2001) also chronicled the historic black working-class struggle for social justice. The researchers discussed interracial solidarity in the labor union and attempted to explain why racial differences may persist within class struggles with a comparison of the interracial unions of the Congress of Industrial Organizations and the more exclusionary affiliates of the American Federation of Labor.

Zeitlin and Weyher (2001) observed that the United States has one of the most diverse working-classes in the world, but this quality has used by capitalist as a wedge to limit the formulate a class consciousness among workers. Workers may view the presence of a racially diverse workforce as a problem to overcome. A racially diverse work force may simultaneously be used as a tool of capitalists to keep workers fighting each other and not those controlling the means of production. The authors examined the ways in which black and white workers dealt with the issue of diversity as they attempted to organize labor. What the researchers found was that "to gain a modicum of job security and protect their wages and working conditions, organized workers are compelled to choose between a strategy of exclusion, which may also take the form of ethnic or racial discrimination, or of inclusion, and class-wide solidarity" (p. 431). While the authors addressed the role of the black working-class in the struggle for greater rights for workers, we critiqued the work for what we found to be the authors treatment of racial discrimination and racial disparities as byproducts of economic products; therefore, race and racism are secondary to class issues.

There was a need to place the labor struggle within a much larger historical context. Zeitlin and Weyher (2001) had this to say about the significance of historical memory, "the suppression of historical memory, whether intentional or not, has pernicious intellectual consequences, for when the past is obscured, the sources of the actual present-and what else was possible-are mystified. Surely the prevailing explanations of the widening white/black unemployment gap provide some important insights. But, because they are ahistorical and depoliticized, they are inherently misleading if not simply false" (p. 461). For "it was in the wake of the decline of the demise of the CIO as a potent organizational expression of interracial working-class solidary that black Americans slipped backward, " argued Zeitlin and Weyher (2001, p. 461).

The black working-class has not only played key roles in the Civil Rights Movement and the labor movement but also in efforts to draw greater attention to the plight of women in American society. In *Journal of Gender Studies,* Lois Weis and Julia Hall addressed the intersections of race, class, and gender, but Horton and I argued, failed to address manifestations of racism in feminism.

Using ethnography, Weis and Hall (2001) explored how poor working-class white females expressed racism in contrast to their white male counterparts. Weis and Hall (2001) found "the ways in which poor and working-class male identity circles around the construction of the viral black male 'other,' discouraging cross-class solidarity in the face of an economy that currently hurts the poor and working-class across race and ethnicity" shape identity formation" (p. 43). The study findings showed that white women verbalized racial prejudice, but did "not exhibit the element as a central part of their identity" (p. 43).

In explaining how poor and white working-class women participate in racism, Weis and Hall (2001) weighed in on the issue about how best to measure social class. The researchers contend that the boundaries between the poor and the working-class are so fluid that researchers must consider both. Despite findings by Thomas Shapiro and others that middle-class status is tenuous—especially for people of color—Weis and Hall (2001) did not make the argument that the boundaries between middle-class and working-class are "fluid, with shifting boundaries, that cannot be isolated from each other easily" (p. 44). While Weis and Hall (2001) raised the prospect that racism can be engendered, they fell short in their failure to distinguish be-tween poor and working-class white males and females and they discussed blacks as if they were classless. Moreover, Weis and Hall (2001) minimized the legacy of racism within the feminist movement, romanticizing attitudes and behaviors between white women and blacks. It is quite possible that engaging in the "othering" of blacks is not a central component of racial and class identity for white women because historically and in contemporary times their racial and class identity was dependent upon their male counter-parts who hold more privilege in the male-dominated society in which we all must live.

Research on race, class, and gender since 2000 not only focused on *doing racism* for poor and working-class white men and women, but research also focused on universities as places of protected white space. France Wind-dance Twine wrote a short essay in 2000 in *Signs: Journal of Women in Culture and Society*. In the essay, Twine (2000) discussed the challenges she-and other faced-as women of color from working-class background as a graduate student and later as a member of the faculty. As a graduate student at University of California, Berkeley in the late 1980s, Twine (2000) was shocked to learn there were "no students of working-class origin, no U.S., blacks, and no American Indians" in her cohort. Twine—who identified herself as black and American Indian—contemplated leaving the university because of "ongoing racism and elitism that prevailed" (p. 1228). As an instructor of sociology, Twine (2000) was surprised working-class U.S. blacks and American Indian were missing from the instructional staff. The lack of representation of working-class blacks and American Indians was only part of the problems on college campuses and universities during the 1990s, but also in the previous decade. Twine (2000) argued the Reagan administration attacked working-class students with dreams of earning a col-lege education. Financial aid decreased during the 1980s, or was altogether eliminated. "Working-class students have much less access to government-sponsored financial support for a university education" (p. 1230).

Twine (2000) identified a host of issues that scholars are continuing to deal with were colleges and universities are concerned. Twine (2000) talked about "patterns of recruitment and hiring that fail to consider how the valorization of scholars who possess class and cultural privilege (as measured by the quality of degrees and letters) undermines the egalitarian ideals" that many colleges, universities, and departments purport to value (p. 1229).

Brunsma et al. (2013) described predominately white colleges and universities as fortresses designed to protect and uphold white supremacy. Colleges and universities are not necessarily sites for the exchange of new ideas. Contrary to the popular images, predominately white colleges and universities are necessarily sites where challenging the racial status quo is encouraged. Institutional policies and procedures, along with daily activities, including teaching and research, are products of processes that create and perpetuate a racialized hierarchical social system within institutions of higher learning and in the broader society.

In making the case that predominately white colleges and universities are places of protected whitespace that are surrounded by walls of whiteness, Brunsma et al. (2013) discussed several important assumptions: 1. Race is a foundational concept in the founding and the development of our nation; 2. Race is a social construction; and 3. Racism affects whites and people of color, but in different ways. Twine (2000) and Weis and Hall (2000) made similar arguments over a decade prior to Brunsma and his colleagues.

THE TRULY DISADVANTAGED: THE BLACK WORKING-CLASS

It is not a coincidence that the black working-class has been at the center of social justice issues for generations. One need only look at data on how blacks in the working-class fare relative to blacks in the middle-class and to whites in the middle- and working-classes on a host of sociological outcomes. The highest level of educational attainment for the working-class is a high school diploma or equivalence, although some measures included individuals with some college.

A comparison of blacks and whites with high school diplomas shows the enduring racial divide that exists and will continue to persist given current trends in education reform and the unequal treatment many people of color face because of their minority group status. According to data collected by the National Center for Education Statistics between 1996 and 2008, the percentages of working-class blacks was greater than the percentages of working-class whites during the same time. Thirty-five percent of blacks were working-class in 1996 and 2000. The percentage of blacks in the working-class increased slightly by 2004 to 36 and declined in 2008 to 35. For whites 34.7 percent were working-class in 196 and 2000. The percentage of whites in the working-class dropped to 32.8 percent in 2004 and 31.6 percent in 2008. Both whites and blacks reported higher percentages of respondents in the working-class between 1996 and 2008 than middle-class, as measured at least a bachelor's degree.

Data from the National Center for Education Statistics (2010) revealed differences by race and gender for blacks and whites in the working-class in 2007, just before the Great Recession. White male workers ages twenty-five and older reported median annual earnings for full-time, full-year wage and salaries of $40,000 compared to $65,000 for similar middle-class white male workers. Black male workers in working-class earned $32,000 and black male workers in the middle-class earned $50,000. The gap between white males in the working-class and black males in the middle-class was $33,000 and the gap between black males in the working-class and white males in the working-class was only $10,000.

By 2008 data from the National Center for Education Statistics (2010) showed that the percentage of unemployed whites in the working-class was 5.7 percent compared to 10.9 percent for blacks in the working-class. Unemployment for whites in the middle-class was 2.0 compared to 3.5 for blacks in the middle-class. Unemployment for whites in the working-class between the ages of sixteen and twenty-four was 12 percent. Unemployment for blacks in the working-class in the same age group was twenty. Whites in the middle-class reported an unemployment rate of 3.9 compared to 6.5 for blacks in the middle-class.

Data was also released by National Center for Education Statistics on the percentage of children ages six to eighteen, by parent's highest level of educational attainment and the child's race for 2008. Based on the numbers released in 2010 we can determine the percentages of children in working-class families. About 26 percent of white children had mother's whose highest levels of education was high school compared to 35.5 percent of black children. A quarter of white children had mothers with at least a bachelor's degree compared to only 12.5 percent of white children. Twenty-seven percent of white children had fathers whose highest level of educational attainment was a high school diploma compared to 35 percent of black children. About 24 percent of white children had a father with at least a bachelor's degree compared to 14.2 percent of black children.

EDUCATION AND THE
WORKING-TO-BOTTOM-CLASS PIPELINE

The black working-class is already disadvantaged when compared with working-class whites and contemporary reforms to public education are already showing signs of exacerbating the observed differences. We should be concerned about the creation, maintenance, and perpetuation of a working-to-bottom-class pipeline. Researchers have already established the fragility of American middle-class, especially the black middle-class, but one could speak of the fragility of the American working-class, particularly the black working-class.

Shapiro and his colleagues include discussed the impact of the Great Recession on the black middle-class. Prior to the Great Recession the black middle-class was less secure than other middle-class Americans. "In the pre-recession period of 2000 to 2006, the percentage of African American middle-class families who were economically secure fell from 26 percent to 16 percent." The researchers identified a host of factors behind the insecurity of black middle-class status. The factors included loss of health insurance, housing burden, and asset poverty. Access to health insurance, a lower likelihood of being housing-burdened, and asset ownership increase as income and education increases so it can be said that if the black middle-class was vulnerable before, during, and after the Great Recession that the situation for the black working-class was even more insecure. One of the main risk factors to financial security is having a high school diploma or less (Wheary et al. 2008).

Educational policies which seek to further divide communities by race and class add to the insecurity of the black working-class and feeds into a working-class-to-bottom-pipeline which plays a role in ensuring that black children in the working-class do not realize their parents' dream that their child will be more successful than they were and instead are kept in the working-class or funneled into a bottom-class where members must rely on public housing, food assistance programs, and may also increase their likelihood of arrest and even incarceration.

The adaptation of the Wal-Mart business model to public education has material consequences for many individuals and groups, but especially for the black working-class. While there are disagreements about how best to measure the black working-class there are other factors that are not in dispute. 1) The black working-class represents a significant proportion of the black population and has for many generations. 2) The black working-class has been at the forefront of the historic struggle for social justice. 3) The black working-class will be most harmed by the current education reform movement because they are even more economically secure than other American social classes, including the black working-class. 4) Current trends in public education helping to move blacks in the working-class through a pipeline that is likely to lead to intergenerational downward social mobility. 5) The experience of intergenerational downward social mobility will provide yet another mechanism for moving historically disadvantaged groups through the prison pipeline. In the next chapter I examine the beneficiaries of the big box approach to public education in America.

Chapter Six

Does Common Core
Make Common Sense?

Existing and proposed changes to public education costs individuals, house-holds, neighborhoods, and the broader society, but educational reform also enriches elites and those with middling authority and privilege. In earlier chapters I discussed education as a growth machine, the big box store model, and the impact of changes to public education on the working-class, especial-ly the black working-class. Here I examine two topics so controversial and impactful that they warrant further consideration. These topics include Com-mon Core and standardized testing. Common Core and standardized testing are controversial in large part because they demonstrate just what can happen when profit, privilege, and privatization replace a concern and a commitment to a public good. Responses to the implementation of Common Core in East Baton Rouge School District in Louisiana are presented here. Louisiana is as at the epicenter of debates concerning Common Core with push back from Republican Governor, and presidential hopeful, Bobby Jindal. I argue that the true crisis of the modern educational reform movement is not only repre-sented in the Common Core and in a culture of high stakes test taking, but the real crisis is in the adaption of colorblind ideology to explain the causes and ignore the enduring consequences of policies which put profit before people.

COMMON CORE STATE STANDARDS AND CONTROVERSIES

Over the past several decades there has been a movement to improve Ameri-ca's public schools. Gaidimas and Walters (1993) described the shift in their article about the roll out of Common Core State Standards (CCSS) in Maine. The authors not that the State of Maine began restructuring public schools in the mid-1980s with financial support from the Smart Family Foundation who made their money as the publishers of Esquire magazine. The focus of the foundation was on education. Maine started with a focus on improving instruction and found that improvements in instruction did not necessarily lead to improvements in overall academic achievement. Maine later moved toward a more integrated framework for curriculum and instruction. The four areas of focus were human record; reasoning and problem solving; communication; and personal and global stewardship. History, reflection, application, use of various media and citizenship were stressed.

Maine unapologetically adopted a business approach toward educational reform, including the use of the quality circles models (Gaidimas and Walters 1993). The quality circles models were used widely in Japanese corporations and later used by many American corporations. The model was intended to give "equal voice in problem solving" (Gaidimas and Waters 1993 p. 32). Lawler and Mohman (1985) described the quality circle models in great detail in their work, which was published in *Harvard Business Review*.

Quality circles replaced suggestion boxes. The suggestion groups provided employees with more input in the decision-making process within a corporation. Quality circles were thought to create a participative culture. Quality circles existed as parallel organizational structures. "To accomplish anything, the circles have to report their results back to the existing organization, which is the object of change as well as the controller of the resources necessary to effect it" (Lawler and Mohman 1985).

According to *The Economist,* quality circles were usually comprised of three to twelve individuals engaged in similar work. These individuals typically met one hour per week on a volunteer basis. Working with their regular supervisor, it was expected that workers would identify issues and present solutions. One latent function of quality circles were to boost morale and create opportunities for workers to discuss issues. Ultimately, the success of the circles depended upon support from senior management. Although widely popular in the 1980s, quality circles were criticized by some as "useless if the company's management was not trained in the more general principles of total quality management." Another criticism was that the idea of quality circles was not modified to reflect American culture. Lawler and Mohman (1985) said, "in more individualistic western societies it became a formalized hunt for people to blame for the problems that it identified. The original intention was for it to be a collective search for a solution to those problems." What often ended up happening was the senior management ignored "real problems raised by staff" and focused on the trivial.

The application of the quality circles model from business to education was an effort to impose a "foreign" structure of governance onto teachers which the goal of assimilating teachers into the ways of those with the true decision-making ability. This is a strategy used not only in the adaptation of business models to education, but in efforts to extract resources from indigenous populations under the guise of power sharing and inclusion. This explains the resistance of teachers in Maine who were apprehensive about the proposed changes despite claims that teachers were involved at all phases of aimed at restructuring schools.

When Maine shifted its focus from instruction to curriculum they again sought support from private foundations and found it with the Danforth Foundation. Danforth Foundation supported educational initiatives nationwide up until the late 1990s when the foundation limited its scope to the St. Louis, Missouri area and began concentrating on the development of plant and life sciences; neighborhood redevelopment; and downtown revitalization. Maine would also receive support from United Technologies and serve become part of John Goodlad's Network for Renewing Schools.

Goodlad's philosophy was that "we will not have better schools without better teachers, but we will not have better teachers without better schools in which teachers can learn, practice, and develop" (www.ieiseattle.org/CER.htm). Goodlad framed education and schooling "in terms of the moral and political dimensions of teaching and learning in a democracy." He viewed education as "an inalienable right in a democratic society and that the purpose of education is to develop individual and collective democratic character." He supported schools that would "support and sustain lifelong teaching careers characterized by professional growth, service, and satisfaction."

Public schools in Maine and across the country have moved away from the aforementioned ways of viewing teaching and learning in recent years. Young and Potter (2014) describe when, why, and how the shift got started and what continues to fuel the change and where we should expect to see movement in the coming years. Young and Potter (2014) argued that the privatization of New Orleans schools after Hurricane Katrina and an increase in corporate interests in education occurred just before the United States entered into what became known as the Great Recession.

A recession occurs when the value of what a nation has to offer decreases over a period of time. Although the United States has experienced a number of recessions throughout the course of the nation's history, the recession the United States experienced in 2008 had a tremendous impact on government, industry, and everyday Americans. "Housing prices were at their peak and within a relatively short period of time fell, leaving many borrowers unable to make good on their loan obligations" (Martin 2013, p. 78). At the same time, "actions on Wall Street were placing the market on the brink of peril" (Martin 2013, p. 78). The Great Recession provided cover for "cost-saving" reforms in public education (Young and Potter 2014, p. 50). While public school budgets were being slashed, initiatives to create a national curriculum emerged. "CCSS were developed under the guise of philanthrocapitalism, the notion that corporate interests can both do good and turn a profit at the same time (Young and Potter 2014, p. 50).

As of July 2013, forty-three states were in the process of implementing CCSS. According to National Public Radio (NPR) Arkansas, Nevada, Texas, and Virginia never adopted CCSS and Indiana, Oklahoma, and South Carolina adopted but later backed out. The standards were designed to establish learning standards for students in elementary and high schools within the public school system to ensure that students were ready or work and college. Many on the left resisted CCSS because of the seeming obsession with testing to measure student success and to evaluate teacher quality. Individuals on the right criticized CCSS and are yet another example of the federal government overreaching its boundaries in a state issue such as public education.

CCSS was to provide to a way to quantify student programs and compare performance across schools and states, which was not possible in previous years. Young and Potter (2014) described how standardized education outcomes formally began in 2009 with the Council of Chief State School Officers and the National Governor's Association forming groups to create English Language Arts and math standards. A validation committee was also established and in record time states were adopting the standards. The Obama Administration provided over three billion dollars in financial incentives for doing so through Race to the Top, but the administration was the not the first to support standards. Young and Potter (2014) said the seeds were planted in the early 1980s. The National Commission on Excellence in Education issued a report in 1983 entitled, A Nation at Risk: The Imperative for Educational Reform. The purpose of the commission, which was chaired by David Pierpont Gardner was to define problems and provide solutions "not search for scapegoats." The commission was charged with identifying the strengths and weaknesses of the American public school system. More precisely the specific charges were: assessing the quality of teaching and learning; comparing American schools and colleges with peer nations; studying college readiness of high school students; identifying best practice models; assessing impact of educational reforms to over the past twenty-five years; and defining problems.

The commission was particularly concerned by what it considered "a rising tide of mediocrity." In particular, the commission was concerned with the ability of Americans to compete with other nations. It was alleged that America "lost sight of the basic purposes of schooling, and of the high expectations and disciplined effort needed to attain them." Part of the problem, as the commission saw it, was the fact that American schools were overburdened. "They are routinely called on to provide solutions to personal, social, and political problems that the home and other institutions either will not or cannot resolve." The commission did not attempt to address the causes for such issues, such as historic public policies because that would be viewed as "scapegoating" as opposed to seriously considering the social and political context in which American public schools functioned historically and in contemporary times. Just before identifying the risks to the nation, the commission observed that when "properly informed," the American people would do what was right for the children. Clearly the commission was prepared to create a narrative about the state of public school. The narrative included concerns about a working force that was at risk of falling behind the Japanese who make automobiles, the South Koreans who built steel mills, and Germans who were excelling in the manufacturing of machine tools. Although the primary focus of the risk factors was on commerce and industry, the report is careful to note that the issue goes much deeper.

"The people of the United States," reads the commission's report, "need to know that individuals in our society who do not possess the levels of skill, literacy, and training essential to this new era will be effectively disenfranchised, not simply from the material rewards that accompany competent performance, but also from the chance to participate fully in our national life." This sentiment is not represented in current debates surrounding educational reform and likely represents how American society should view education and not how education was actually viewed.

Nevertheless, the commission's report included several power statements, which bear repeating. "The report noted, "For our country to function, citizens must be able to reach some common understanding of complex issues, often on short notice and on the basis of conflicting or incomplete evidence." Drawing from the words of Thomas Jefferson, the 1983 report to President Reagan included the following, "I know no safe depository of the ultimate powers of the society but the people themselves; and if we think them not enlightened enough to exercise their control with a wholesome discretion, the remedy is not to take it from them but to inform their discretion." The report also noted that "All, regardless of race or class or economic status, are entitled to a fair chance and to the tools for developing their individual powers of mind and spirit to the utmost. This promise means that all children by virtue of their own efforts, competently guided, can hope to attain the mature and informed judgment needed to secure gainful employment, and to manage their one lives, thereby serving not only their own interest but also the process of society itself."

Education was not viewed as a form of workforce development as it is conceptualized in contemporary times. As one reads through the document, it becomes clear that the commission also loses site of those powerful words. All of the deficiencies identified are discussed in the context of business needs. "The demand for highly skilled workers" was the driving force behind the document.

The commission acknowledged the frustrations many felt (and feel) with respect to parents, teachers, and community leaders. The frustrations are set to cut "across ages, generations, races, and political and economic groups." The commission wars against "the unproductive tendency of some to search for scapegoats among the victims, such as beleaguered teachers." The commission was clearly attempted to avoid discussions about the legacy of public policies on school reform movements and in doing so is adopting a color-blind approach to discussions surrounding educational reform where there are clearly problems with the public education system but few are willing to acknowledge their role as beneficiaries.

The report "informs almost all efforts to reform failing schools in the last thirty years; its focus on the importance of a competitive workforce is reflected in the man corporate and corporate friendly donors and supporters" (Young and Potter 2014, p. 52). High profiled individuals in the business community wrote the document. The same criticisms levied against the 1983 document are being levied against CCSS. Young and Potter (2014) said, A Nation at Risk "can be understood as a privately sponsored education crisis narrative and the CCSS as a largely privately funded response in the form of a nation-wide education reform effort" (p. 52).

No Child Left Behind shined a spotlight on the desire and/or need for higher and clearer state standards, but there was a great deal of variation in the standards. Standardization is at the heart of CCSS. Plans to require testing-based assessment are "viewed as both NCLB-derived and pedagogically unsound means of assessment and evidence of the money-making motives of the creators of the CCSS" (p. 55).

Despite commonly held beliefs, CCSS does not dictate curriculum, but "efforts already exist to standardize the paths schools take to meet the CCSS" (p. 55). Additionally, there are particular concerns about the conflicts of interests that exist given the money to be made from testing and curriculum development to meet the demands of CCSS. Bill and Melinda Gates are at the core of the controversy surrounding such conflicts. The creators of CCSS, David Coleman, Sue Pimental and Jason Zimba, to invest in promoting and developing CCSS, recruited Bill and Melinda Gates. The Gates Foundation invested over $200 million to the effort and expedited a process that usually takes years to just a few months. Aligning research and advocacy, "the Gates Foundation distributed millions of dollars of grants for research to develop and support the CCSS at the same time that is spent millions of dollars to promote them to state and federal officials, teachers, unions, and business entities" (p. 56). The strategy employed by the creators of CCSS and the Gates Foundation reflected a larger trend in education philanthropy, which "is for the biggest donors to fund an overlapping set of organizations that promote approaches and entities that compete with institutions of public P-12 education. These incentives range from the promotion of charter school expansion of online/technology-based education programs to alternative teacher-education programs like Teach for America" (57).

The Gates Foundation also provided resources to implement Measures of Effective Teaching (MET), which used what is called value-added modeling or VAM. VAM is "designed to measure educational progress independent of external factors in the environment of the student" (57). The focus is on improvements from one testing period to the next. Throughout the country as much as half of teaching evaluations in some states relies on VAM, which some researchers have found is methodologically flawed. However, data derived VAM have found their way to very important places, including in the justification of the California ruling on teacher tenure in the *Vergara v. California* case of 2014.

Diana Ravitch has written extensively of problems in CCSS and with broader movements. Not only is CCSS used to vilify teachers but it also, like NCLB, provides teachers with an incentive to "teach to the test." Scandals in places like Atlanta are some examples. The consequences of the measures to reform public schools are numerous and include lower the moral of teachers; closing public schools; opening privately managed charters and the increasingly presence of "a burgeoning educational industrial complex of testing corporations, charter chains, and technology companies that view public education as an emerging market." Improving education and creating equal opportunities are not the main concerns, argued Ravitch, "but everything to do with cutting costs, standardization education, shifting the delivery of education from high-cost teachers to low-cost technology, reducing the number of teachers, and eliminating unions and pension." A former supporter of CCSS, Ravitch changed sides once she become aware that there were no field-testing and the overall "lack of any democratic participation in their development." Additionally, the absence of an office responsible for addressing concerns was noteworthy for Ravitch.

Missing from much of the discussion around CCSS is the existing and long-term effect on historically disadvantaged groups. There are some notable exceptions. For example, one recent study conducted by the National Urban Research Group (NURG) suggests that the educational system in the United States is unfair, particularly toward economically disadvantaged Black and Latino students (Singer 2014). The NURG took the Common Core math assessment scores from Spring of 2013, and found that the percentage of New York City public middle school children from minority and poorer families who scored below proficiency level increased. African American students' proficiency dropped by 30.5 percent between 2012 and 2013. This does not mean that white students' proficiency did not drop, their proficiency decreased by a lesser degree; it dropped from 79.2 to 49.6 in sixth grade math proficiency between 2012 and 2013.

NURG found that certain socio-economic factors predicted student success. These factors included family income and race. Over three-fourths of students with disabilities, regardless of race, scored "Below Standard" on their seventh grade ELA and math tests. English Language Learners had similar results (Cody 2014).

The huge drop in proficiency was not unsurprising. Kentucky, the first state to adopt the Common Core State Standards in 2010, saw proficiency rates drop by nearly a third the first year. It is difficult to tell when the scores will rise again. Indiana has dropped the program entirely (Rich 2013).

Passing the Common Core may become incredibly important if states begin to require it to graduate. In New York, the current implementation plan is for the class of 2017 to be required to pass the Common Core exams to graduate high school. If this becomes a requirement, private tutoring will grow and will be utilized by more affluent students (Hacker and Dreifus 2013).

Most states have implemented the standards within the last school year, and data is not available about the effects of the Common Core on their test results or on their students' individual achievement.

THE UNHOLY TRINITY:
RACE, CLASS, AND THE COMMON CORE

My colleague Catherine Lowe and I wrote and presented a paper at the Annual Meeting at the Southern Sociological Society in Charlotte, North Carolina on the intersections of race, class and school reform in the spring of 2014. We focused on Louisiana, especially the East Baton Rouge School District given tensions between the state's governor and others concerning the implantation of CCSS. In our work, we observed the following. After Hurricane Katrina, the United States watched in horror as families in poverty were stranded for days in the Superdome or in their flooded neighborhoods. Most were shocked at the abject poverty in New Orleans. Jason De Parle wrote days after the storm hit that, "What a shocked world saw exposed in New Orleans last week wasn't just a broken levee. It was a cleavage of race and class . . ." (DeParle 2005). Louisiana was known for the city of New Orleans, and that city was known for its music, its food, colorful politicians, and Mardi Gras. The depths of poverty and the extensive history of racial discrimination that affect the entire state were rarely seen by visitors.

Poverty and racial discrimination in New Orleans and Louisiana were not novelties, and have made an impact for generations on the lives of children in the state. Despite the integration of schools in the 1960s, twenty-four parishes are still under federal desegregation orders. Public schools in largely minority areas have poorer achievement rates. In metro areas, public schools are majority minority, with many white students attending private schools. These instances of de-facto segregation have separated students by race and socioeconomic status. A controversial school voucher program, the Louisiana Scholarship Program, led to the state of Louisiana to be sued by the Department of Justice for "impeding desegregation."

As much of life in Louisiana is governed by socioeconomic status and race, especially education, this paper seeks to discuss the relationships among class, race, and poverty in regards to education and student achievement. Public school teachers, who work in the classroom each day with the affected students, were the chosen participants, and were interviewed about their experiences.

LOUISIANA EDUCATION: A HISTORICAL PERSPECTIVE

The Catholic Church provided the majority of educational opportunities for children in Louisiana during the colonial period in Louisiana; this education was given without charge if a family was unable to pay. Because of the vast nature of the Louisiana colony, many of the children of the French and Spanish colonists remained illiterate (Cline 1974).

The first movement for public education in the Louisiana colony began during Spanish rule, under Governor Luis de Unzaga in 1772. His plan for public schools in New Orleans, supported by public funds but run by Spanish priests led to discontent and little support from the French settlers (Cline 1974).

Slaves could not be educated under Louisiana state law. Free black children, including Creole children, were educated at home, in private schools, or in parochial schools. Some light-skinned African American children "passed for white" (*passer pour blanc*) and attended public school (Bankston and Caldas 2002).

It was not until 1847 that the state of Louisiana instituted a statewide public school system, an action spurred by the adoption of the 1845 state Constitution, which called for a system of free public school. Funds were distributed based on the number of children, ages six to sixteen, to be educated by a district, which was made up of at least forty students. Despite the abolition of state funding to private schools with this new law, private schools continued to receive state funding in regions where public schools did not exist (Harris 1924).

Louisiana seceded from the Union in 1864; Union forces quickly took New Orleans in 1862 (Cline 1974). General Butler's administration ran the local schools during the continuation of the war, while the Freedmen's Bureau established schools for children of color in all areas taken by the Union army. Of the 15,000 eligible children of color, 8.000 were enrolled in schools and were instructed by over 125 teachers (Harris 1924).

After the adoption of the 14th amendment, it was legally required that public schools educate both white children and children of color, a change reflected in the 1868 state Constitution. For the next decade, white children enrolled in private schools or did not attend (Cline 1974).

In 1871, Lieutenant Governor Oscar J. Dunn enrolled his three African American daughters at the Madison Girls' School, an all-white school. Eleven boys were educated that same year in two white schools in New Orleans (Amistad Collection 2014). When an African American girl was accepted to a girls' high school in New Orleans at the end of Reconstruction, the city rioted for three days and resulted in the death of a man and child (Bankson and Caldas 2002).

Parish school boards began to re-segregate schools in 1877, and by 1898, schools were entirely separate. There were 2,221 white schools, and 982 schools for children of color. Teachers in white schools were paid one hundred dollars more than their counterparts in schools for children of color (Cline 1974).

DESEGREGATION

Jim Crow laws governed every facet of life in the South and segregated residents of Louisiana. When *Brown v. Board of Education* mandated integration of schools, and 1964's Civil Rights Amendment passed, Louisiana was slow to accept the changes. New Orleans residents were outraged when four African American girls, including Ruby Bridges, began first grade at McDonogh No. 19. The Louisiana Legislature passed a resolution commending white parents who had withdrawn their children from the school at the admittance of these students. In 1961, Louisiana Governor Jimmie Davis threatened to close down the entire New Orleans school system instead of allowing a single African American student to attend a white school. With the grace of Judge Wright of New Orleans, desegregation continued on a one-grade-a-year basis ("History of the Federal Judiciary" n. d.). Faculty desegregation did not begin in Louisiana schools until 1967-1968 (Public Affairs Research Council of Louisiana 1969). fifty-five out of sixty-six Louisiana public school systems had some student desegregation at the beginning of the 1968-69 school year. The nine that remained segregated were not under court order (Public Affairs Research Council of Louisiana 1969).

Although districts used busing and other measures to desegregate schools, the increase in "white flight" to private schools has led to an increase in majority of minority students in many Louisiana public schools.

THE RECOVERY SCHOOL DISTRICT

Before Hurricane Katrina devastated southeastern Louisiana in August 2005, 90 percent of New Orleans public schools received performance grades below the state average. Twenty-nine school officials were indicted for fraud and corruption by the FBI in 2002. The hurricane damaged all but sixteen school buildings in the city, and the state legislature voted to take control of the schools. By establishing the Recovery School District (RSD), the legislature fired 7500 teachers and school workers. The RSD includes schools in New Orleans, seven schools in Baton Rouge, and three schools in neighboring parishes. Many of the formally public schools became charter schools. Five schools in New Orleans are still run by the Orleans Parish School Board (Kay 2013).

Because many families and students were displaced across the country during the evacuation process, they experienced high-quality school systems and returned to the New Orleans/Baton Rouge area with higher expectations for their schools. Local leaders are working to create equitable schools for all students, regardless of socioeconomic status or race (Washington, Smith, Jones and Robinson 2008).

RACE AND POVERTY IN LOUISIANA

Louisiana is rarely rated positively in any comparative state-by-state ranking. It has one of the highest rates of poverty in the country: 26 percent ("Poverty Rate by Race/Ethnicity" n. d.). Half of the parishes in the state are considered "persistently poor." 15.7 families experience food insecurity and just over 404,000 children benefit from SNAP (USDA 2012) In 2012, the overall poverty rate was 26 percent. Poverty is divided by race: 44 percent of Louisiana African Americans were poor, compared to 17 percent of white Louisianans. Hispanics, a significantly smaller portion of the Louisiana population (4.5 percent), had a poverty rate of 35 percent ("Poverty Rate by Race/Ethnicity" n. d.). Whites who are in poverty in Louisiana still have more opportunities than most African Americans in the state, especially in the realms of education, income, and life expectancy (Burd-Sharps, Lewis and Martin 2009).

Louisiana has historically held one of the highest child poverty rates. In 2013 Louisiana was 47th in child poverty with a rate of 29 percent, representing over 317,000 children. Disparities among racial lines begin at birth. The infant mortality rate for Louisiana nonwhite infants is 13.6, slightly higher than that of Russia and Bosnia (Burd-Sharps, Lewis and Martin 2009). In comparison, Louisiana white infants have an infant mortality rate of 6.1 per 1000 live births. 25 percent of Louisiana's children live at less than 100 percent of the Federal Poverty Level. 22 percent live at 100 percent–200 percent of the Federal Poverty Level (Louisiana Kids Count n.d.). A third of children were living in households with a "high housing cost burden" (Louisiana Kids Count n.d.). Over half a million children in Louisiana receive free or reduced lunch (Children's Defense Fund 2013). 65,000 children were without health insurance in 2013, despite the implementation of the Affordable Care Act and Louisiana's LaCHIP program, which covers children of low-income adults whose income is too high to qualify for Medicaid. 45 percent of children live in single-parent households (Louisiana Kids Count n.d.).

Louisiana's child poverty is also divided by race. While 14 percent of white children in the state are poor, 47 percent of black children in the state live in poverty.

Baton Rouge, the state capital, ranks 11th in "concentrated poverty" when compared to metro areas in the years 2005–2009 in Brookings Institute Data (Ward 2011).

In terms of human development, Louisiana is ranked thirty years behind states such as Connecticut; in other words, Louisiana citizens live as the average American lived in 1990. The life expectancy, educational opportunities, income, and infant mortality rates in Louisiana can be compared to those of the rest of the United States in the early 1990s (Burd-Sharps, Lewis and Martin 2009).

Income inequality has grown in Louisiana, and is among the states with one of the highest income inequality, with a rate of 8.8 percent. The richest Louisianan households have average incomes just over fourteen times as large as the bottom 20 percent of households. This phenomenon is also characterized racially: white Louisianans earn an average income of $28,912 a year, African Americans in the state earn just over $17,000. Both African American and white women earn less than their male counterparts, although they are more likely to have attained higher education (Burd-Sharps, Lewis and Martin 2009).

EDUCATION AND RACE IN LOUISIANA TODAY

It has been suggested that schools in low socioeconomic areas and high-minority population schools cause lower academic achievement in students due to social segregation (Bankston and Caldas 1998). African American students in schools find social attitudes that tell them they are expected to fail (Epps 1995). In the push for standardized testing in schools, African American children have been found to fall behind white children as early as kindergarten (Epps 1995). Several studies report that minority student achievement is directly linked to teacher confidence in the student (Irvine and York 1993). Minority students are three times more likely to be suspended and expelled from schools than their white counterparts. This includes preschool children—almost half of all preschoolers who are repeatedly suspended are African American. They are also more likely to attend schools where one-fifth of teachers do not meet state teaching requirements (Rich 2014).

Despite the decision of *Brown v. Board of Education* nearly sixty years ago, racial integration has not been achieved in many schools in Louisiana (Hacker 1992). While East Baton Rouge is no longer under federal desegregation orders, but twenty-four other Louisiana parishes are ("Judge: Voucher Law, Tangipahoa Parish Desegregation Order Conflict" 2012) In 2007, East Baton Rouge was released from federal desegregation supervision after a court case that began in 1956, ending the longest federal desegregation case in the nation (Eggler 2007). In Baton Rouge, most public high schools are majority minority, and those that are not are home to magnet or gifted programs. Private schools are majority white, and three of the four local Catholic high schools have a student body that is over 90 percent white. Stephan Caldas, a former professor at the University of Louisiana-Lafayette, said of this, "If this was all about desegregating schools, it didn't work. The consequences were pretty much the opposite of what we want: The middle class left, took all of their social capital and financial capital, and moved to the middle-class parishes that surround them" (Eggler 2007). In the case of Baton Rouge, parents sent their children to private schools or formed their own independent school districts, as in the cases of Baker, Zachary, and Central. See Tables 6.1 and 6.2 for a breakdown of the racial composition of selected schools in the Baton Rouge area.

A new debate in East Baton Rouge education is the possible creation of a breakaway city, St. George. This proposed community would include over 107,000 current residents of East Baton Rouge parish. In the proposed area, 74 percent of the current voters registered are white, compared to 42 percent in the city of Baton Rouge. The original plan for the new city would have increased the percentage of black students in East Baton Parish Public Schools from 81 percent to 86 percent (Samuels 2013). Another plan in the East Baton Rouge School district is the possible creation of four separate districts: Southeast, North Baton Rouge, Mid City, and South Baton Rouge. Each district would have a deputy superintendent, overseen by the EBR superintendent. The plan, Bill SB484 introduced by state Senator Mack Bodi White, Jr, has at the time of this writing, been introduced in the state Senate and referred to the Committee on Education (Samuels 2014).

We interviewed six ESL specialists in the East Baton Rouge School District. Because of the volatile political nature of education in East Baton Rouge schools and the state government's historical practice of firing teachers who disagree with policy, it was difficult to find content area teachers

Table 6.1.   Racial Composition of Selected Schools in Baton Rouge Area: 2012–2013

Schools in Baton Rouge Proper	Public or Private	% African American	% White
McKinley Senior High School	Public	84%	13.20%
Baton Rouge Magnet High School	Public Magnet	41.90%	44.90%
Belaire High School	Public	81.30%	12.90%
Broadmoar High School	Public	80.20%	13.80%
Glen Oaks Medical Magnet	Public Magnet	99.20%	0.60%
Scotlandville	Public	99.20%	0.80%
Tara High School	Public	83.80%	14.10%
Woodlawn High School	Public	61.20%	35.80%
Catholic High School (boys)	Private	2.90%	96.20%
Episcopal High School	Private	8.90%	85.80%
Redemptorist	Private	39.80%	54.50%
St. Joseph's Academy (girls)	Private	4%	92.50%
St. Michael the Archangel	Private	2.70%	94.10%

Source: Author generated table based upon data from education.com

willing to participate. The ESL specialists who did agree to be a part of this study had a unique view of education in the parish, as many have taught English and Language Arts and move from school to school.

ESL specialists answered nine open-ended questions regarding race, class, and poverty in their classrooms. These questions were guided by our five research questions:

1. How has the practice of "tracking" affect students' self-perceptions and their achievement?
2. Although numerous students have proven that high-stakes tests are biased toward white, middle class students, are teachers aware of this?

Table 6.2.   Racial Composition of Selected Schools in Baton Rouge Area: 2012–2013

School	Public or Private	% African American	% White
Baker High School	Public	91.50%	7.30%
Central Community High School	Public	14.70%	83%
Zachary High School	Public	43.40%	53.80%

Source: Author generated table based upon data from education.com

3. Do educators use multicultural materials and teach multiple perspectives in their increasingly diverse classrooms?
4. Are educators aware of the effects of poverty on their students?
5. Have teachers themselves seen or experienced institutional racism or classicism in their schools?

Four of the six specialists were white, with one choosing not to respond. All were women and the average age was 46.5 (two chose not to respond). The average years employed in the district was seven years (one chose not the respond). Three lived where they taught. Three were married. Four had completed work beyond a B.A., or were in the process of completing a Master's degree.

The six teachers were asked nine questions regarding the Common Core State Standards, barriers to student achievement, multicultural education, racism and classism in schools, and biases in high-stakes testing:

1. How have Common Core State Standards affected your classroom?
2. The practice of "tracking" students has historically led to the placement of a disproportionately high number of low socio-economic and minority students of low-socio-economic and minority students in special education classes and "lower-track" classes. Does your school utilize tracking? If so, has there been any impact on students' achievement or self-perceptions due to placement?
3. Are student's home and school environment linked? If yes, what factors of a child's home environment impact their achievement? If not, why not?
4. What are barriers to student achievement?
5. Do you find high-stakes testing to be devised based on what the average white, middle class student would know or be familiar with?

Table 6.3.   Change in the Racial Composition of Selected Schools in Schools in Baton Rouge Including Proposed St. George Community: 2008–2013

	2008		2013	
	White	Black	White	Black
Baker	33%	64%	25%	73%
Baton Rouge	45%	51%	42%	53%
Central	93%	5%	91%	7%
St. George	78%	17%	74%	20%
Unincorporated	32%	65%	29%	69%
Zachary	66%	31%	62%	35%

Source: Author generated table based upon data from education.com

6. How do you incorporate multicultural education, or the incorporation of histories, cultures, and traditions from groups that are not typically represented in textbooks or educational materials?
7. Have you seen or experienced institutional racism or classicism in your school? Please cite some examples
8. What sort of support is available for poorer economically disadvantaged students? Does your school offer any type of programs other than federally subsidized free breakfasts and lunches?
9. Do you have anything else to add?

RESULTS

Opinions about the Common Core State Standards were mixed. All respondents spoke of the differences in lesson planning that the new standards required. Respondent 1 said that the new skills and approach required by the Common Core is "difficult to teach on a daily basis because students . . . are resistant to [it]." Because Louisiana did not have a specific curriculum before this, Respondent 3 said that teachers are more thoughtful in their lesson planning because of the clear requirements. For Respondent 4, the Common Core has negatively affected her students because it has negatively affected classroom teachers. "Teachers are not sure what some of the standards are or how to teach them. . . . I am scrambling to find additional ways to teach the information to my ESL students who aren't getting the information the first time" (Respondent 4). A similar situation is occurring in Respondent 5's schools: "[It] has instilled an aura of tension into teaching and learning." . . . The differences in experiences may be due to the variety of schools the ESL specialists work in.

Few schools utilized tracking; many of the respondents working solely in elementary schools. Respondent 4 mentioned that the parish is encouraging students not to be evaluated for special education classes, due to the time the process takes and the amount of paperwork. She finds "the ESL students who need to be in special education are being pushed on from grade to grade 'because of their language' instead of looking at each child and doing what is best for him/her."

All ESL specialists believed that a student's home and school environment are linked. Several respondents mentioned the level of parental expectations, level of familial literacy, value placed on education at home, parental encouragement, and parental apathy all directly impacts their students. Some children "fall behind" when they are "tired and hungry and don't want to be in school" (Respondent 4). Those who are achieving in this specialist's class have parents who are active in their child's school life. She acknowledges, however, that there are parents who work "ungodly hours."

The respondents had varied responses in regards to barriers to student achievement. For English Language Learners, the barriers were multiplied: some students had insufficient instruction in their first language, educational gaps, new cultural context, and the added complication of not having daily, specialized language instruction (Respondent 2). Respondent 3 believed that for some female students, there are cultural differences "toward the value of education and training," which harms educational instructional. Students may not have access to books or materials for assignments. Because of the constant stress to meet new testing standards, teachers must teach the curriculum, and "don't have time to give extra help to those who really need it" (Respondent 4). Several respondents mentioned apathy: parent, student, and teacher apathy. Respondent 1 wrote that, "The policies need to go beyond assumptions about young people in disadvantaged communities having low inspirations. Instead, it should tackle barriers to fulfilling them, with tailored policies for particular areas."

High-stakes testing were generally thought to be biased towards white, middle class students. Respondent 2 referred to them as "culturally very biased." One suggestion, from Respondent 3, was that the questions should be "for geographical area and experiences students have had or would be familiar with, not so much referring to class or race." Some respondents believed the tests have become more culturally aware in recent years; Respondent 4 wrote, "the math and science are okay, but do see social studies and reading passages to be somewhat biased." The sections with the most reading have not improved. Only one respondent, (Respondent 5), believed the tests are based "on what an average educated person would know." Differences in opinion may be based on the experiences in particular schools, as the socioeconomic and racial makeup of the individual schools where each ESL specialist teaches is different.

Multicultural education practices varied on each particular school. Some individual classrooms utilized multicultural educational practices, while some entire schools encouraged the sharing of cultures not typically represented in textbooks. Respondent 4's ESL department hosts "culture days" where international speakers give talks on their country and students participate in games. One of her schools makes announcements in Spanish and Arabic, the two other languages represented at that school. Respondent 5 personally used videos, stories, and articles that she chose that had minority perspectives in her classroom. One of the schools where Respondent 3 is placed pairs ESL students with a "buddy" and the ESL student talks to that buddy about his or her culture and language. Respondent 1 said that for teachers to implement multicultural education in their classrooms, they must "be open to their students and put forth the effort needed to get to know their students inside and outside of the classroom."

Four respondents reported racism and classicism in Baton Rouge public schools. Students make fun of the clothes and food of people from different countries, use insulting language about particular ethnic groups, and tell jokes directed at particular groups in the schools where Respondent 1 teaches. Respondent 2 reported racism toward Hispanic students. Respondent 4 has heard administrators and teachers "tell parents who don't speak English that they need to learn how to speak English since they live in America." In faculty meetings at certain schools, the faculty segregates racially. She has also seen "adults and students react negatively to dirty, disheveled children. Teachers don't want to hug or talk much to them. . . ." Respondent 5 said she had experienced some reverse discrimination form parents, students, and some administrators. Respondent 6 said she "would be very surprised to have experienced institutional racism or classicism. . . . In the 5 schools I've worked all but one of the principals were minority, and most of the faculty and staff were minority."

Most schools offer some type of extra support for economically disadvantaged students. Free hearing and eye screenings were offered at Respondent 2's school. Respondent 4's schools have aftercare programs whose cost is based on a sliding scale according to income. She "has seen teachers pay the field trip fee for students who couldn't afford to pay them." The district wide program ICARE is present in all schools, but Respondent 5 mentioned that students "rarely take advantage of [it]." Non-profits such as City Year, Boys and Girls Club, and Freedom School are in several area schools.

Only one ESL specialist responded to the last question. Respondent 5 spoke about the key to student achievement, which in her opinion is a caring adult. Regardless the socioeconomic status of the child, she said caring adults—either family members or teachers—are who inspire students to succeed.

Because ESL specialists work with predominately minority children in smaller classrooms, they had a view that was unique to this discussion. All of them taught in public schools, and all of their schools are majority minority.

A great deal of emphasis was placed on apathy—student, parent, and teacher. Teacher apathy was linked to teacher burnout. It was unclear if teacher apathy and burnout were also linked to the mentioned lack of respect for authority. Student and parent apathy may be caused by their socioeconomic situation.

The ESL specialists mentioned students and parents were not aware of many of the support programs available to them in the local schools. Several of these programs—free hearing and eye tests, afterschool care, and tutoring—would be of great benefit to students if communication were not a barrier. Further research on why community programs are not communicated and publicized in both the ESL and mainstream community is needed.

Louisiana adopted the Common Core State Standards in 2010; it was not until the 2013–2014 school year that schools began implementing the curriculum. Each district and type of school was able to adapt their curriculums in a different fashion. For example, St. Tammany Parish educators revised their online curriculum themselves while East Baton Parish proposed hiring outside experts from Pennsylvania. (NOLA implanting common core) As testing results from Louisiana are available in the coming year, it will be interesting to see how the specialists' perceptions match the proficiency scores of local students.

Tracking did not seem to be a phenomenon in East Baton Rouge Parish Schools. Most of the respondents were aware that high stakes tests were culturally biased, although two believed they have improved in recent years. All of the teachers used some form of multicultural education in their classrooms or in their schools. Their emphasis on multicultural education may have been related to the populations they taught: predominately minority and English Language Learners. Few specialists directly mentioned poverty in their statements. The barriers mentioned by each specialist and the individual issues mentioned in regards to a student's home environment alluded to poverty. Several of the specialists had seen and experienced racism and classicism in their classrooms and schools, the most egregious being the faculty racially segregating themselves in one teacher's school during faculty meetings. Other respondents had not seen racism and would have been "surprised" had it occurred. One respondent even said she experienced "reverse racism" from students and parents.

The differences in responses from ESL specialists mark the difference in experiences based on where teachers are placed and the geographic location of that school.

These respondents were aware of the effects of poverty and race on their students, but did not mention that poverty and race could be a cause. They mentioned their students were hungry and tired from taking care of their siblings, but did not discuss the *why*. The reasons for not naming the reasons for the problems their students have is not defined.

Education in Louisiana is highly political, and has been since it began during the colonial period. Decisions made about state scholarship programs, vouchers, and teacher readiness, are all based in politics, and it was difficult to find any educators willing to discuss these difficult issues during such a politically charged time. Because of the rapidly changing education system in Louisiana, further research will be needed as separate school districts are created within the city. If the secession movement succeeds and the city of St. George becomes a reality, we will need to know how the further de-facto segregation will affect our students.

CCSS is the latest in a long line of efforts to restructure the public school system in a way that maintains the status quo. Unfortunately, maintaining the status quo not only means the continuation of privileging the wealth, but it also means the continuation of the suffering of far too many people of color, especially blacks. The alleged colorblind nature of CCSS has material consequences. While philanthrocapitalists and others are focused on preparing the workforce of today and of tomorrow people of color are by and large being kept out of positions where they can wield influence. Blacks are continuing to his glass ceilings, glass windows, glass doors, glass escalators, and glass elevators. Far too many blacks are stuck on a conveyor belt or proverbial treadmill moving along, but not really going far. For all the talk of getting children prepared for college and the world of work, the fact of the matter remains that even with the right set of academic tools, black children are far less likely to have the resources to be able to go college and are far more likely than white children to graduate with a relatively high income to debt racial. Even the most qualified black job applicant faces discrimination at virtually every stage of the hiring process from where jobs are advertised (if advertised at all) to whether an applicant with a "black sounding name" is even contacted for an interview. Blacks do not receive as great a return on their investments into education as whites and other degree holders and this is true on a host of sociological outcomes.

I recently gave a talk as part of a lecture series sponsored by the Curriculum Theory Project at Louisiana State University and I highlighted differences between blacks and whites with bachelor's degrees between 2000 and 2012 and the findings are quite revealing. I analyzed data from the American Community Survey, which is generously made available by the University of Minnesota.

The percentages of white and black college graduates who owned their own homes increased between 2000 and 2012 but a much larger percentage of white college graduates owned homes compared to black college graduates in both years. The percentages of unemployed college graduates increased for blacks and whites between 2000 and 2012. However, the percentages of unemployed blacks were nearly double the percentages for whites. Average incomes declined for black and white college graduates between 2000 and 2012. In each year blacks earned substantially lower than whites and there was less variation in incomes for black college graduates than for white college graduates. On average, whites with at least a bachelor's degree reported interest, dividends, and rental income that were more than five times the value for blacks with the same educational attainment. Housing values, on the other hand, increased for black and white college graduates between 2000 and 2012, but homes owned by whites with at least a bachelor's degree were worth more than homes owned by blacks with at least a bachelor's degree. The following figures show the stark contrast between blacks and whites with at least a bachelor's degree compared with others.

The connection between the business community, philantrocapitalist, and elected officials is dubious at best. The creation of a crisis for the purpose of generating profits for some at the expense of others is reprehensible and regrettable. Even those who opposed CCSS are acting not out of genuine concern for the children, largely children of color in rural and urban communities, but on their own agendas. Conservatives are using the educational plight of children of color in their tug of war with the Obama Administration and their ongoing belief in the supremacy in state's rights, which historically has made it easier for local areas to treat people of color unfairly. Similarly, you have liberals opposing CCSS not because of the disproportionate harm to the poor and to children of color but as a form of resistance to the current administration and those in the business sector placing demands on groups who had assumed that they had some degree or privilege or at least middling authority and sudden found themselves being told what to do and how to do it. Lots of competing agendas and interests with little focus on the current and lasting impact of CCSS on the poor and communities of color. There are those who get it, but they are in the numerical minority and are often marginalized and suppressed on both ends of the political spectrum. The real crisis is in the continued unequal treatment that students of color endure, as they are more likely to attend schools deemed failing. Students of color are also more likely to face disciplinary actions for discretionary actions. Students of color who manage to beat the statistical odds will more likely than not experience racial discrimination as they seek employment, attempt to purchase a home or other real estate, and even risk being frisked or killed for simply being. The absence of race-specific language is not a prerequisite for determining the deleterious impact a policy will have on a particular racial group. CCSS is currently harming students of color and will continue to harm others if permitted to proceed as is. The likelihood America will change course on public education is not great given the levels and ways some are benefiting from the crisis narrative. In the next chapter we will address one of

Chapter 6

Table 6.4. Descriptive Statistics for Blacks and Whites At Least 25 Years of Age with At Least Four Years of College, 2000–2012

	2000		2012	
	Whites	*Blacks*	*Whites*	*Blacks*
Percentages				
Owner	79.1%	62.7%	80.7%	66%
Renter	20.9%	37.3%	19.3%	34%
Married	61.7%	39.2%	61.3%	38.4%
South	31.7%	54.6%	35.5%	57.9%
Employed	77%	79.1%	71.6%	74.2%
Unemployed	1.4%	2.1%	2.5%	4.4%
Not in the labor force	21.6%	18.9%	25.9%	21.4%
Mean (Standard deviation)				
Total household income	$123,739.81 ($113,924.04)	$86,861.66 ($68,611.99)	$116,421.85 ($104,625.62)	$81,742.81 ($69,699.42)
Age	48.26 (14.85)	45.68 (13.73)	52.68 (15.71)	50.19 (14.53)
Interest, Dividends, and Rental Income	$8,400.59 ($31,585.08)	$1,381.32 ($9,088.16)	$6,510.26 ($29,153.08)	$1,203.99 ($11,370.47)
Housing Values	$297,054.78 ($241,709.31)	$196,344.72 ($160,468.11)	$352,420.10 ($414,945.62)	$223,788.15 ($244,172.73)
N	35,337	2,265	306,968	24,556

Source: Author generated table based upon analysis of American Community Survey for 2000 and 2012.

the key reasons for the lack of high profile resistance to CCSS by communities most affected: that reason is the role of plutocrats in displacing indigenous organizations and educational leaders.

Chapter Seven

Plutocracies and the Displacement of Indigenous Organizations and Educational Leaders

Democracies are founded upon the radical idea that power is best entrusted to the people. When one person, one vote is no longer the lynchpin around which democracy pivots and wealth corrupts power, then a state is not democratic, but is more reflective of a plutocracy. Several scholars contend the United State is a plutocracy, in whole or in part, as evidenced in the amount of power and influence possessed by a relatively small group of individuals and corporations that hold a majority of the nation's wealth. The dominance of wealthy elites has many consequences is evidenced and achieved in many ways, including by controlling the media and dictating public policy. The dominance of wealthy individuals and corporations is evidenced in other important and somewhat understudied ways. Plutocracies often lead to the removal of indigenous individuals and institutions in ways that minimizes the ability of historically disadvantaged communities, such as the black community, to master change, as evidenced in the work of Kanter (2003). To demonstrate the connectedness of plutocracies and the black community, we begin with a discussion on the characteristics of plutocracies. Next, we discuss several of the most significant indigenous institutions in the black community and their role in ensuring access to a quality education for all children, including black children. Then, we address the effects of actions plutocracies on significant institutions in the black community.

PLUTOCRATS: RULE BY THE WEALTH

Plutocracy is a term that has been a part of the American lexicon for centuries, but has recently come into vogue in the wake of concerns about financial contributions and the idea that some businesses are simply too big to fail. Harry Adams wrote about plutocracies in an article published in *Constellations* in 2008. Adams (2008) defined plutocracies as "states that are ruled unfairly by corrupt, wealthy elites" (p. 126). Adams (2008) clarifies the definition by noting that all systems of law and government are susceptible to corruption and may be motivated by private gain. In some cases, governments may be "hard-wired for corruption, so that their leading institutions are systematically geared to support unfair dealings. Accordingly, we might distinguish predominately just states-that suffer from only occasional, isolated episodes of corruption-from predominately corrupt states-that suffer from this regularly, as a pervasive, systematic disorder" (p. 126).

Contemporary plutocracies obtain and consolidate their power "through three salient channels—through media, electoral, and legislative institutions that otherwise form the heart of a fairly and properly function democracy" (Adams 2008, p. 128). Control of the media is important in a plutocracy. He who controls the media controls the public conversation. When a plutocracy is in place, the media's role is to "convey news items and content that was either neutral towards or supportive of, but seldom critical of, the sponsoring elite" (p. 128). Among the major consequences of the control of the media is to degenerate "free speech and public discourse, along with open and accurate news" (p. 128).

Some might argue that evidence of elite domination of the press is long standing, but even more apparent in recent years. According to *Business Insider,* six corporations controlled all but 10 percent of the media in America in 2011. Lutz reports that in the early 1980s, 90 percent of American media was owned by fifty companies. The six companies included GE, News-Corp, Disney, Viacom, Time Warner and CBS. GE's notable properties, included: Comcast, NBC, and Universal Pictures. Notable properties owned by News-Corp, Wall Street Journal, and New York Post. ESPN, ABC, Pixar, and Miramax were all Disney properties. Time Warner controlled CNN, Time, and HBO, while CBS's notable properties included NFL.com, 60 Minutes, and Showtime. The article also showed that "232 media executives control the information diet of 277 million Americans."

Moreover, the findings showed that the aforementioned six companies controlled 70 percent of cable television. News Corp owns the top newspapers on three continents. Despite efforts on the part of the Federal Communications Commission (FCC) to limit the number of stations one company can own, Lutz (2012) reported that Clear Channel owns over 1,000 stations, where 80 percent of stations' playlist match.

FCC consolidation regulations, according to Gail Mitchell, were in part responsible for the decline in black owned media. Mitchell (2013) said, despite black consumer power and ability to see products "one key voice is slowly and systematically being silenced. That African-American communities across the country are losing a vital means of local engagement." Black medial ownership has declined since the mid-1990s when the minority tax certificate was repealed by Congress and the Telecommunications Act of 1996 became law and permitted broadcast companies to own as many radio stations as they could afford. The number of black companies owning radio stations fell from 146 in 1995 to 68 in 2012. Moreover, companies where blacks spend lots of dollars do not advertise in black owned newspapers and other news outlets.

In addition to the media, "the electoral process would become co-opted in a plutocracy" (Adams 2008, p. 128). Those with the greatest access to the media and wealth and those willing to following the directors of their financial backers who get the exposure needed for success in political campaign. Individuals with less resources, limited access to the media, and an absence of big corporate sponsors, "regardless of how reasonable their campaign platforms might be, would largely be kept out of the public eye. The only candidates who would make it through the primaries would thus be well-heeled individuals who represented the vested interests of those already well-off, and those who could convince wealthy contributors that they would act faithfully on their behalf, particularly if their interests conflicted with the interests of other non-wealthy parties, who were not able to give as generously to their campaigns" (Adams 2008, p. 128). Adams describes the number of unfair tactics that might be used to ensure the outcome of particular races from "wealth candidates making deals with voting machine companies to rig their machines (as Diebold was accused of), drawing up unfair redistricting plans (as Tom DeLay was indicted for), and simply preventing voters from voting, in counties where they would be much more likely to vote for populist and anti-plutocratic candidates (by providing insufficient numbers of machines, falsely categorizing voters as felons, creating unnecessary traffic, hold ups and so forth, as happened to thousands in Florida counties in 2000), would apply here as well. Through tactics such as these, the principle of "one dollar, one vote" would effectively come to replace the democratic ideal of "one person one vote" (Adams 2008, p. 128–129).

Since 2000 there were reports of efforts to disenfranchise voters, especially black voters. Limiting "Souls to the Poll," cutting short early voting days, introducing and passing voter identification laws, and Supreme Court decision which weakened the power of Section V of the Voting Rights Act of 1965 are some other examples of what Adams and others witnessed during prior elections.

Sachs (2014) puts it this way, "Pity the American people for imagining that they have just elected the new Congress. In a formal way, they of course have. The public did vote. But in a substantive way, it's not true that they have chosen their government." Sachs describes the election as "the billionaire's election." Although some billionaires supported one of the major parties over the others, "what unites them is much stronger than what divides them" (p. 1). Regardless of the apparent gridlock and bipartisan nature of Washington, Sachs says there is actually very little polarization. America's political system is reflective a strong sense of solidarity for the super-rich. "There has never been a better time for the top 1 percent. The stock market if soaring, profits are high, interest rates are near zero, and taxes are low. The main countervailing forces—unions, antitrust authorities, and financial regulators—have been clobbered," writes Sachs (2014, p. 1). The political system is bought and paid for by four big lobbies: "Big Oil, Wall Street, defense contractors, and medical care giants" (Sachs 2014, p.1). It is hard to quantify how much big lobbies put into the latest election because of favorable decisions by the highest court in the land, but Sachs (2014) says "that the Koch Brothers, through their complex web of shell groups, put in at least $100 million and probably much more. Many other billionaires and corporate contributions helped to raise the total amount spent on the 2014 midterm elections to $3.6 billion. Unfortunately, those elected to represent the people far too often vote the interests of their donors, not the society at large" (p. 2).

Despite efforts to register black voters, black voter participation is low in some areas and the many blacks live in areas where the majority of elected officials are non-black. According to the Pew Research Center, black voter turnout in midterm elections is traditionally lower than white voter turnout. For example in 1986 voter turnout was 50.7 percent for whites and 45.6 percent for blacks. By 2010 white voter turnout was 48.6 percent and black voter turnout was 44 percent.

Additionally, a report by Shala Dewan (2014) the *New York Times* revealed "mostly white forces in mostly black towns." In Maple Heights, Ohio the Cleveland suburb went from predominately white to about 75 percent black over a thirty-five year period. The fire department has no black firefighters and of the thirty-five police officers, only two are black. Dewan (2014) also showed that there are places like Maple Heights, Ohio throughout the United States. "Nearly 400 departments, most with fewer than a hundred officers, were substantially whiter than the populations they served. In these departments, the share of white officers was greater than the share of white residents by more than 50 percentage points." Dewan (2014) focused on Ferguson, Missouri, the site of the killing of an unarmed young black male named Michael Brown, which set off days of protests. With a population of about 20,000 people, the black population in Ferguson increased over the past few decades, but Ferguson and Maple Heights "have white mayors and largely white political leaderships."

According to Adams (2008), the corruption of the legislative and fiscal processes is essential to any plutocracy. "Biased legislation would consequently be passed that all too consistently favored corporate interests over and against community and worker interests" (p. 129). Green (2012) argued that the relationship between corporate elites and legislators has gotten even stronger over time as the financial industry has become an even greater part of the American economy than in previous eras.

Green (2012) described what he called "the rise of financial plutocracy." The financial industry is among the most important because all other social institutions must rely on it. "The dependence gives real power to the elites who run financial institutions, but the transformation of the industry over the last forty years has resulted in a concentrated power far out of proportion to the rest of corporate America" (p. 118). As financial firms collected greater shares of all corporate profits, the "firms grew in significance, many of their executives developed close revolving-door relationships with regulatory agencies, and their firms inundated Congress and the executive branch with cadres of lobbyists" (p. 118).

The perceived and actual corruption of the legislative and fiscal processes has eroded the public trust, argued Green (2014). There were five key ethical failures: 1) pervasive and acute conflicts of interest arouse in the incentive relationships between rating firms and investment banks and thrifts, between some regulatory agencies (such as the Office Thrift Supervision) and he regulated firms; 2) the lack of transparency among the firms, regulators, and clients at all levels contributed to the ethical malaise; 3) the lack of transparency was exacerbated by lax or nonexistent report requirements, outright falsification of faces reported on many documents, and the eroding attention to due diligence in collecting and verifying solid information about loans and securities; 4)the recalcitrance of banks, thrifts, and investment firms toward examiners in some regulatory agencies was abetted by the examiners' own agency managers, leading to immense frustration and low morale in the ranks; and 5) the almost complete disregard among so many of these highly trained and paid professionals for any sense of public trust (pp. 123–124).

Plutocrats not only chip away at the public trust, but one could argue that plutocrats attempt to manipulate the public trust through their philanthropic work. Barkan (2013) described, "how big philanthropy undermines democracy" (p. 635). Barkan (2013) wrote that big philanthropy started in early 1900s with foundation such as, Russell Sage, Carnegie Corporation, and the Rockefeller Foundation. Unlike other charities "they had vastly larger assets, they were structured legally and financially to last forever, each was governed by self-perpetuating board of private trustees; they were affiliated with no religious denomination; and they had grand, open-ended missions along the lines of improve the human condition. They were launched in essence as immense private corporations dealing in good works. They would pay no taxes on endowment income, property, or donations: they would do good and they would intervene in public life with no input from or accountability to the public" (p. 635). These new charities were viewed as "centers for plutocratic power that threatened democratic governance" (p. 635). The main purpose of the charities was not to promote a public good. The main purpose was "to secure wealth and clean up the reputations of business moguls who amassed fortunes" (p. 635).

Barkan (2013) made the argument that one hundred years after these charities emerged that their goals are to address social issues and their board of trustees determines what issues are problems and how to fix them. "They may act with good intensions, but they define "good." The arrangement remains thoroughly plutocratic: it is the exercise of wealth-derived power in the public sphere with minimal democratic controls and civic obligations" (p. 636). The public subsidizes the philanthropic efforts of plutocrats by way of such things as tax-exempt status. What Barkan (2013) calls "big philanthropy" is continuing to grow and that growth is not necessarily good for everyone. "Mega-foundations are more problematic now than in the twentieth century—not only because they have proliferated but also because of the political, economic, and social context in which they operate: the cult of the market, the drive to privatize public provision, an increased concentration of wealth in the top 1 percent, celebration of the rich for nothing more than their accumulation of money, inadequate government resources for public goods and services, unlimited private financing of political campaigns since the Supreme Court's Citizens United decision, and an unenforced (perhaps unenforceable) separation of the legal educational activities of nonprofit groups (including foundations) from illegal lobbying and political campaigning. In this context, big philanthropy has too much clout" (p. 638). For more than ten years big philanthropy has set it sites on public education with funders such as The Bill and Melinda Gates Foundation, the Eli and Edythe Broad Foundation, and the Walton Family Foundation at the helm (Barkan 2013).

Several of the Obama Administration's most vocal critics use the term plutocracy to describe the favorable policy responses wealthy individuals received following the Great Recession, particularly in comparison to policy aimed at lifting Americans out of poverty. Dr. Cornel West's comments describing President Obama as a "black mascot of Wall Street oligarchs and a black puppet of corporate plutocrats" received a lot of attention (Thompson 2011). West appeared with Tavis Smiley on Morning Joe before a discussion at George Washington University on the subject of "Remaking America." Smiley and West were asked why politicians do not talk about the poor. Smiley responded by laying the blame squarely at the feet of both political parties. Smiley argued that the suffering of the poor was not present in the political arena. Reflecting on the presidential debates of 2008 between then Senator Barack Obama and Senator John McCain, Smiley observed that the candidates or the moderators never mentioned the words "poor" or "poverty." MSNBC flashed data from the U.S. Census Bureau for 2010, which showed the number of individuals living in poverty in 2009 at 43.6 million and 46.2 million in 2010. The lack of attention devoted to the poor, according to Smiley, was proof positive that the poor didn't count and that the poor didn't matter. West argued that poor people in America were not a priority because "big money is in the driver's seat." West cited the Occupy movement for drawing attention to the economic divide in the nation. West said that it was only when the poor and "people of good consciousness organize" that politicians will show concern of the poor. Smiley described the poor as the new poor, who were formerly in the middle-class, the near poor and the perennial poor. West was later pressed by one of the guests about the impact of the Affordable Care Act, a signature of the Obama Administration, and the impact of expanding health care coverage on the poor. West reluctantly admitted that the policy would help struggling Americans, but called upon the administration to do more. When asked whether Republicans presented a better alternative West conceded that the party the president was "better than the mediocrity of Republicans but that is not saying a lot." West concluded that the system itself is broken.

MSNBC host and professor, Melissa Harris-Perry responded West's characterizations of President Obama in *The Nation.* Perry said West "criticized President Obama's economic and social policies and painted the president as cowardly and out of touch with black culture." Perry in turn criticized West's comments as "more personal than ideological," and added that the comments "gave insight into the delicate ego of the self-appointed black leadership that has been largely supplanted in recent years" (Harris-Perry 2011). In an effort to end the back and forth between West and Harris-Perry supporters and opponents Harris-Perry wrote the following:

> Whatever the accuracy or erroneousness of West's remarks, there was little new in them. Argument about the corporate control of American politics, the ascendance of Wall Street over Main Street and the imperial impulse to American foreign policy have been the standard talking points of the left for more than a decade. What fascinated the press were the salacious tidbits offered by West that suggested black-on-black infighting (Harris-Perry 2011).

The focus of the debate between West and Harris-Perry was primarily on whether or not the comments were justified and not on the impact of corporate influences on the black community over many Republican and Democratic administrations. West and other critics of President Obama's policies were either less vocal and/or given less attention when directed at previous presidents who were of course all white males. Whether the attention given to West's critique of President Obama is indeed "a battle royal" akin to that described in Ralph Ellison's *Invisible Man* as Harris-Perry argued, the fact of the matter remains that corporate influences in American government have had a tremendous impact on blacks and that the influences did not begin and will certainly not end during the two terms of the nation's first black president.

What is ironic is that while some on the far left like Cornel West assign the label of plutocrat to President Obama, some self-proclaimed plutocrats have used the term "hate" to describe their feeling toward the Commander-in-Chief. In discussions about her book, *Plutocrats: The Rise of the New Super-Rich and the Fall of Everyone Else,* Freeland notes "that there has been a real shift away from Barack Obama, and a lot of these guys loved him in 2008. They saw him as one of us. Right? He was a self-made guy. And they feel really angry at Obama, and it's not just about the question of taxes, although that angers them a lot" (NPR 2012). Freeland added that what is happening in America is that the lines between personal business success and public virtue are less defined. "And in a certain extent, your moral and civic virtue could be measured by the size of your bank account" (NPR 2012). Freeland says the super right want to be good as well as rich and successful.

Nick Hanuer (2012) responded to Leeland (2012) and others for their critique of plutocrats in *Business Insider,* which may read like an article in *The Onion.* In a not-so-widely publicized TED Talk, Hanuer described himself as a plutocrat and as a capitalist. He viewed the talk as an opportunity to talk to other plutocrats, or as he put it, "to his people." He stated that he has invested in over thirty companies across varying industries. He was the first non-family investor in Amazon and sold a company to Microsoft for $6 billion. "My friends and I won a bank," he added. He added that he was a capitalist and that like most plutocrats he had a broad perspective on business. He let those in attendance know that they have no idea what being a plutocrat is like. He said he owns a plane, a yacht, multiple homes, and so forth. He claimed to not be the smartest or the hardest working guy but because of "birth, circumstances, and timing," he has enjoyed success. He also attributed his success as a venture capitalist to a high tolerance for risk and an intuition about the future, which he identified as the hallmark of any good entrepreneur.

What does the future look like according to Nick Hanauer? With the wealth, power and income more concentrated in the hands of the 1 percent, Hanauer sees "pitchforks." He sees a move from American capitalism to an economic system akin to eighteenth century France. The problem is not that there is some inequality. "Some inequality is necessary for a high functioning capitalist democracy," he added. He called upon his fellow plutocrats to leap outside of their "gated bubble world," before it is too late.

In the *Business Insider* piece, Hanauer (2012) says, "the growing economic distance between people like me and the little people like you hasn't been this great in a long, long time. You may call it inequality. We call it freedom." He says the little people "need to get with the program." He then goes on to explain his "distain" for President Obama, and says other plutocrats feel the same way. "We hate him because his views about the importance and primacy of the middle-class diminish our status. The threat he represents isn't economic; it's existential. It's not just our pocket books that are threatened, but also more importantly, our prestige and our influence in this country. Our manhood is at stake."

Hanauer (2012) goes on to state what he considers some simply truths. He argues that people's beliefs are based on a number of things, but facts or evidence is not one of them. Hanauer (2012) says believe "what makes them feel good. And what makes us feel good is a set of beliefs that reinforce our status, privileges and power." The 99 percent simply must come to grips with the following, "we plutocrats matter. It also means that you don't matter." Haunauer (2012) does wish to do something about economic inequality.

Dylan Matthews (2013), writing for the Washington Post says, Hanauer supports raising the minimum wage to keep the pitchforks at bay, but his economic rationale for doing so is not supported by existing research. Matthews (2013) writes,

> There's a case to be made that mild increases in the minimum wage are worth it, either because one doesn't believe in employment effects or because one believes the wage increases it causes are worth it. But Hanauer's proposed increase is recklessly large and even supporters of minimum wage hikes don't think it's a serious option. If he wants to help poor workers and not subsidize corporations, then he should advocate expanding the Earned Income Tax Credit and funding it with a new tax on corporations. It could be a carbon tax or a payroll tax or a cash flow tax or a profits tax or a tax on capital income - whatever. That's the efficient way to accomplish his goals.

Corporate influences on American politics and other areas of social life resulted in a host of issues including the removal of indigenous individuals and institutions by limiting their effectiveness to master change as defined by Kanter (2001).

Kanter (2001) described change masters as "people who know how to conceive and lead productive and effective projects, initiatives, or ventures that bring new ideas into use" (p. 1). Kanter (2001) also wrote, "there are a generic set of skills found in the people who lead successful change efforts" (p.1). The skills outlined in Kanter's (2001) work embodies the features of the historically black institutions that provided the leadership for social justice movements throughout the nation's history, but have been weakened by the effects of the increasing influences of corporations which seek to replace

these power institutions and/or co-opt their leadership and render them impo-
tent.

Seven essential leadership skills were identified in Kanter's work (2001).
The first skill involves the ability to identify needs and opportunities. Change
masters "sense a need." Leaders focus "time and attention on the things
going on in the environment." Moreover, "change masters sense problems
and weaknesses before they represent full-blown threats. They see the opportunities when external forces change (p. 1). Historically, leaders of indigenous institutions possessed their skills and used them to empower others and
bring about change. As the size and number of free black communities
emerged during the enslavement era, free black recognized the need for
schools for black children. Free blacks equated education with freedom. The
unwillingness of the broader society meant there was a need for schools for
black children and a need for black teachers. Free blacks saw the opportunity
to not only create schools to educate black children, but to create schools that
would train black teachers. Even after slavery ended, black organizations
recognized the limitations of the Freedman's Bureau and Reconstruction and
thus the leaders of black organizations established mutual aid societies and
other organizations to assist blacks in reuniting families. Blacks started independent churches, not only for the purpose of meeting the spiritual needs of
blacks, but political and economic needs as well. Even before the adoption of
the Thirteenth Amendment, which ended slavery, a group of black clergy met
with General Sherman to discuss the needs of ex-slaves and the clergy,
knowing the environment and sensing the needs of the people, advocated for
the acquisition of land, which led to Sherman issuing Special Field Order
#15. The order, although later revoked, set aside forty acres for each ex-
slave's household and included the use of an old army government mule.

Another important skill change masters possess is the ability to think in
creative ways. Kanter (2001) called this skill kaleidoscope thinking. "Change
masters challenge prevailing wisdom. They start from the premise that there
are many solutions to a problem and that by changing the angle on the
kaleidoscope, new possibilities emerge" (p. 3). Two of the most well-known
black leaders in the late nineteenth century and much of the first half of the
twentieth century highlight possessed this skill. Once slavery ended there
was a great deal of uncertainty. Blacks and whites were unsure how the
country would move forward. Some people, including Abraham Lincoln,
advocated the emigration of blacks to countries in Africa or the Caribbean.
Others sought ways to maintain control over blacks and to limit blacks as
competitors in the market place, for example. Booker T. Washington and
WEB DuBois both believed that blacks could enjoy success in this country
but both had very different, yet creative ways of addressing the issues, particularly where education was concerned. Washington believed blacks would
eventually be assimilated into American society if they learned certain skills

and focused on their economic standing and less on their access political power and areas of public accommodation. DuBois also sought to "shake up reality a little, to get an exciting new idea of what's possible, to break through the old pattern and invent a new one" (Kanter 2001, p. 3). DuBois would not be satisfied with second-class citizenship. He would not be satisfied with accepting racial segregation in some areas of life for the sake of inclusion in other areas. DuBois called for, and worked toward, expanding opportunities for blacks in all areas of social life. For DuBois, "education is that whole system of human training within and without the school house walls, which molds and develops men." For Washington, "at the bottom of education, at the bottom of politics, even at the bottom of religion, there must be for our race economic independence."

Throughout American history the black population has used creativity to address social issues. It would take a number of visionaries to see a day where black and white children could attend the same schools at a time when efforts to resistant the integration of schools and the broader society were met with violence and legislative maneuvering to resist change.

A third required skill for mastering change is the ability to share a vision that inspires and mobilizes people towards a common goal. Leaders "share ideas into a theme that makes a completing case for the value and direction of change" (Kanter 2001). Again, people of African ancestry have demonstrated this skill in a number of ways from the liberal to the most radical thinkers. Social movements involving blacks in America enjoyed success because the leadership was able to make a case based not only on the plight of people of color but on the shared humanity and God-given rights possessed by every man, woman, boy, or girl should. Frederick Douglass made such a case in his speech on the Meaning of the Fourth of July. He envisioned a time in the near future where slavery would end and the dehumanization of people of color would end. He argued for the humanity of the enslaved and the free black population and foretold of the end of slavery. Martin Luther King, Jr. and the hundreds of thousands of people led protests and registered blacks to vote in hostile environments either communicated and bought-in to a vision of what American should and could be and thus responded in kind and joined the legions of foot soldiers who brought about a number of legislative victories. The parents of the Little Rock Nine and the many nameless children who were the first to integrated formerly all-white schools responded to a vision that got "people excited about something they had never seen before," something that did not exist (Kanter 2001, p. 5). Likewise, leaders like Stokely Carmichael and Malcolm X also had a vision for black America and for the world that most thought impossible, a world where people of color would actively resists threats to their lives and exert their independence, personhood, and agency without fear of retribution and by any means necessary.

Kanter (2001) describes four other skills to mastering change. Change masters must also enlist backers and supporters; build and nurture teams; keep going despite setbacks; and celebrate progress. Historically, blacks developed coalitions from within and without. The black population was always diverse racially, ethnically, and economically, but developed important formal and informal ways to work together to bring about change. Migration of blacks from the South and from the Caribbean preceded the Harlem Renaissance, protests surrounding the Scottsboro case, efforts to integrate the military and yet blacks from worked together to bring about positive social changes. The black population has also been very diverse economically. Elite blacks and economically disadvantaged blacks understood that each were subject to the use of the law as a form of social control as evidenced in the number of lynchings, race riots and land takings which took place during the early part of the twentieth century and nonetheless, blacks joined together and worked toward the common goal of ensuring that blacks enjoyed all of the rights they were entitled to as citizens of the United States. Blacks have also developed coalitions with individuals and groups external to the larger black community. Abolitionism eventually became an interracial movement. Blacks and non-blacks joined together to oil the Tuskegee Machine created by Washington. An interracial group founded one of the longest civil rights organizations—the National Association for the Advancement of Colored People (NAACP). The Scottsboro case reignited an interracial commitment toward social justice. A quarter of a million of people from different racial, ethnic, and religious backgrounds made the pilgrimage to Washington, DC to fight for jobs and justice.

Building face-to-face relationships is one critical way to "nurture the working team" (Kanter 2001, p. 9). Indigenous institutions like the black church, the black family, and black schools were historically the centers of both public and private life for blacks in America. These institutions were places where social interactions occurred. Within the safety of the black church, the black family, and black schools, the work of the larger black community took place. Each institution served as a reminder of what was at stake and provided comfort for weary warriors. Meeting in churches, in homes, and in black schools, helped those involved in social movements throughout the course of our history to receive support. They provided opportunities to remind people involved about the goals, challenges, needs and opportunities which was especially important when movements could not point to measurable successes by still needed to keep people interested and mobilized around a cause that was much bigger than themselves.

The black church, the black family, and black schools were also places where everyone who was part of the larger groups goals would be acknowledged and celebrated. "Recognition is important not only for its motivational pat on the back but for its publicity value; the whole organization and maybe the whole world now knows what is possible, who has done it, and what talents reside in the community gene pool" (Kanter 2001, pg. 14). The Tuskegee Airmen understood this. They understood that they success as fighter pilots was not only their success but that it was another nail in the coffin of a racial ideology which claimed, among other things, that blacks were inherently inferior to whites and too cowardly to fight. The victories of the Tuskegee Airmen were not theirs alone. Likewise, Jackie Robinson's integration of modern day baseball was not just about his ascension into an all-white baseball league, but it represented the realization of a revision of a more just and a more equitable society that generations of black visionaries worked towards achieving.

The black family, the black church, and black schools were filled with rituals where black leaders and the followers were acknowledged when ignored by others. In the case of the black church this is especially true. Individuals regardless of their color, social class, occupation, gender, age, and so on, who find places to lead and this often times meant leading those considered to have a lower social rank than one's own self outside of the sacred four walls. The contributions of members, both big and small, were routinely acknowledged in Sunday morning services, which often involved fellowships with area churches. Men's Days, Women's Days, Pastor's Anniversary Day, and various other days of appreciation were meant to allow the church and the community to take a moment and pause and reflect on the contributions of one or more members or groups. The ritual of celebration extended beyond individual churches to the larger community and in other indigenous institutions.

Within the black family opportunities to celebrate members and the unit as a whole went far beyond holidays on the calendar but toward achievements of both children and adults. Family reunions often include celebrations of the lives of ancestors and recognition of individuals who have reached various milestones be they birthdays, graduations, military service, retirement, and so forth.

Celebrating the collective history of people of African ancestry could be seen in churches, families, and schools, three hundred and sixty-five days of the year. Churches would often celebrate the founding of their own churches and denominations which including hanging pictures and an annual reading about the history of the respective church and or denomination. In recognition of Black History Month, Martin Luther King, Jr. Day, Kwanzaa, and in the days leading up to midterm and presidential elections, churches would celebrate the contributions of men and women who sacrificed so much for blacks and for the nation. Black schools would also share this rich history not only during the month set aside for it but daily and by virtue of the existence of teachers and administrators who were from the community and possessed not only the institutional memory associated with each school but that of the larger community as well. There was little need for a Negro History month or a Black Studies curriculum when such materials were incorporated into the everyday experiences and activities of black church in schools. The black church, the black family, and black schools played important roles in mastering change and this was especially critical at times when the dominant narrative claimed the inferiority and inhumanity of black people. The black church, the black family, and black schools countered such claims in their daily operations. These institutions provided a safe haven from the mistreatment and misrepresentation faced by blacks in the larger society. What has happened as the corporate influences have continued to permeate every aspect of society is that the strength of these institutions to continue to serve in these important and history roles has been weakened.

What black leaders have discovered is that their abilities to act as change masters are often constrained by a host of factors that weaken the ability of indigenous institutions to be the change they seek and in many the historic pattern of playing the game using the oppressor's handbook set many leaders and their followers up for failure. My colleagues and I discussed these very issues in a special issue of *Equity and Excellence in Education.*

Kenneth Fasching-Varner, Roland Mitchell, Judge Karen Bennett-Haron and myself address the ways in which the educational and justice systems work "to disenfranchise many (predominately people of color) for the benefit of some (mostly white), based on economic principals of the free market" (Fasching-Varner et al. 2014, p. 410). We introduced a new concept we called educational and penal realism based about Derrick Bell's (1992) concept of racial realism. Bell (1992) defined racial realism as ways of thinking that "requires us to acknowledge the permanence of our subordinate status. That acknowledgement enables us to avoid despair, and frees us to imagine and implement racial strategies that can bring fulfillment and even triumph" (p. 374). Educational and penal realism allows us to move away "from idealism and a false sense of change" (Fasching-Varner et al. 2014, p. 413). We supported our claims by outlining the way in which the prison-to-school pipeline thrives and failure and intentionally undermines the abilities of indigenous communities to control their own destinies in meaningful ways.

We began with a discussion of some numbers that are all too familiar to most Americans. We noted that the U.S. has the dubious distinction of being the prison capital of the developed world. With more than 2 million people in its jails and prisons, the U.S. incarcerate rate is the highest in the world. The racial disparities in the likelihood of incarceration were presented in our discussion of the prison-to-school pipeline. We observed, "although blacks comprise about 13 percent of the U.S. population, nearly 40 percent of people in state or federal persons were black in 2012" (Fasching-Varner et al. 20014, p. 413). Black men and black women, we noted, were significantly more likely to be incarcerated than white men and white women. We showed that grown in the prison population over the past several decades occurred, "not because of growing crime rates, but because of changes in sentencing policy that resulted in dramatic increases in the proportion of felony convictions resulting in prison sentences and in the length-of-stay in prison that those sentences required" (Austin et al. 2007, p. 1).

The impact of mass incarceration on individuals, families, and communities is well documented and addressed in our work in the special issue of *Equity & Excellence in Education.* Children with incarcerated parents did not thrive academically in the same way as children of non-institutionalized parents and black children are much more likely to have an incarcerated parent than white children. A 2012 Sentencing Project report found that black children were more than 7 times more likely to have a parent in prison when compared with white children.

The stigmatization associated with time spent in the criminal justice system has material consequences for all involved. "Under the Welfare Reform Act of 1996, people convicted of felony drug crimes can no longer receive Temporary Assistance for Needed Families. A history of incarceration also limits housing options. Public housing authorities can deny access to public housing to individuals convicted of a drug-related crime or a violent crime based on the Violent Crime Control and Law Enforcement Act of 1994" (Fasching-Varner et al. 2014, p. 414). We though Lynch and Sabol (2004) said it best, the large-scale incarceration of hundreds of thousands of American citizens (who are disproportionately black) "may be underminding . . . institutions of social control such as families and communities (p. 268).

The mass incarceration of so many people of color not only impacts the ability of the historically disadvantaged groups to police themselves, but it also impedes their ability to acquire the most valued resources in society-wealth, status, and power. We can see this in the ways in which mass incarceration perpetuates racial income and wealth inequality and black asset poverty. We pointed to a report by Pew Charitable Trust, which discussed the hidden costs of being an ex-offender. According to the 2010 report, "incarceration depresses the total earnings of white males by 2 percent, of Hispanic males by 6 percent, and of black males by 9 percent (p. 4). Of course income and wealth are not the same. We argued that "the racial wealth gap and the overrepresentation of Blacks among the asset poor can only get worse as blacks, especially black males, continue to be incarcerated in such great numbers, and for longer periods, than in any other time in our history" (Fasching-Varner et al. 2014, p. 415). Data from the U.S. Bureau were provided to show just how wide the chasm is between blacks and whites where assets are concerned. Similar conclusions can be drawn from data from other sources, including from Pew Research.

Drew Desilver (2013) wrote the report, "Black incomes are up, but wealth isn't" and in it he stated that for the past fifty years, "household-income growth for African Americans has outpaced whites. Median adjusted household income for blacks is now 59.2 percent that of whites, up slightly from 55.3 percent in 1967 (though in dollar terms the gap widened). Desilver (2013) observed in the report that "those gains haven't led to any narrowing of the wealth gap between the races." The median net worth for black households in 2011 was actually lower than in 1984. Net worth for white households actually increased by some 11 percent during the same time period. Moreover, Desilver provides evidence that "high-earning married black households have, on average, less wealth than low-earning married white households."

Much of the average American's overall net worth is found in their homes. Blacks tend to have even more of their assets in their homes than whites, although homes owned by blacks appreciate less than homes owned by whites. Looking beyond housing, Desilver (2013) found that racial disparities were even greater on business ownership. "Equity in business was the second-biggest asset class among white households, accounting for 18 percent of average assets, and grew 106 percent in value between 1983 and 2010. Among black households, however, business equity accounted for less than 4 percent of assets on average, and actually lost value between 1983 and 2010" (p.1).

Wealth equals opportunity (McKernan et al. 2013). Mass incarceration has limited the ability of a large segment of the black population to participate in wealth being because they have literally been locked out of the process, thus, limiting access to assets not only for themselves but for those around them. While there are many economic costs to incarceration, there are many benefits too. Fashcing-Varner et al. (2014) discussed the economic benefits of incarceration. Fasching-Varner et al. (2014) argued,

> While it appears unnatural and irrational to want to incarcerate individuals, doing so in ways that disproportionately impact populations considered by the dominant factions of society to be with value eliminates that segment of the population from accessing the wealth of the dominant group. Such an approach also creates an industry (infrastructure, employment, and market) in keeping those "undesireables" away from wealth and access. In essence, those in prison do not simply help maintain the balance of wealth and power, they actually serve to create larger differences between the "haves" and "have nots" (p. 416).

To guide a new way of thinking about the relationship between one's disadvantage position and the system, Fasching-Varner et al. (2014) set forth several tenets "that will help those committed to change to renegotiate the ways in which they approach reform while calling for and shedding a more direct light on those committed to profit in the name of change" (p. 420). First, change masters must come to the realization that "there is no crisis in schools or prisons-each institution is functioning per their design and the demands of society" (p. 420). Second, we must let go of the idea that schools and prisons will reflect the interests of historically disadvantaged grounds and instead with seek to preserve and/or expand the privileged position of members of the dominant group. The third tenet involved the need for people concerned about social justice to be uncomfortable with the present arrangement which involves "both the illusory progress given under the liberalist integration fantasy, and the realities of anti Black racism, black poverty, and blacks' vulnerability to white interests' as seen in schools" (Curry 2008, p. 43). Moreover, "economic imperatives are the central driving force in decisions to sort and separate the marginalized from the oppressors both in education and correction" (Fasching-Varner et al. 2014, p. 421). Furthermore, one need only look at the concentration of wealth among the few in attempts to explain the experiences of historical disadvantaged groups, including blacks, throughout the nation's history.

Educational and penal realism also involves understanding that relationship between the prison industrial complex and seemingly unrelated and race-neutral public policies. Fasching-Varner et al. (2014) said Brewer and Heitzeg (2008) said it best when they argued the following:

> the prison industrial complex is a self-perpetuating machine where the vast profits (e.g., cheap labor, private and public supply and construction contracts, job creation, continued media profits from exaggerated crime reporting, and crime/punishment as entertainment) and perceived political benefits (e.g., reduced unemployment rates, "get tough on crime" and public safety rhetoric, funding increases for police, and criminal justice agencies and professionals) lead to policies that are additionally designed to ensure an endless supply of "clients" for the criminal justice system (e.g., enhanced police presence in poor neighborhoods and communities of color; racial profiling; decreased funding for public education combined with zero-tolerance policies and increased rates of expulsion for students of color; increased rates of adult certification for juvenile offenders; mandatory minimum and three-strikes sentencing; draconian conditions of incarceration and a reduction of prison services that contribute to the likelihood of recidivism; collateral consequences-such as felony disenfranchisement, prohibitions on welfare receipt, public housing, gun ownership, voting and political participation, and employment-that nearly guarantee continued participation in crime and return to the prison industrial complex following initial release. (Fasching-Varner et al. 2014; p. 421)

For many students of color, especially students of color in urban environments, the training they receive is not to prepare them for college or for the world of work; rather, the training is to prepare them to contribute to the self-perpetuating system that is the prison industrial complex. "This training is as import to the welfare of the free market as is training the future presidents, scientists, and businesspeople. The separation and sorting of classes and people is reified through schools and recycled through prisons" (Fasching-Varner et al. 2014, p. 423).

Fasching-Varner et al. (2014) included another important tenet of educational and penal realism and that is that even actors who challenge the system may find that they are contributing to the perpetuation of the every injustices they seek to remedy because "even those with genuine interest in change operate within the landscape of educational and correctional racism and classism" (p. 423).

Schools and prisons play important roles in maintaining the status quo and a result, "populations of color and those of poor socioeconomic standing will continue to be offered up in a serve of the historically and contemporarily overrepresented particularly through schooling and corrections efforts" (Fashcing-Varner et al. 2014, p. 423). We concluded with two final tenets, which point to the significance of understanding the difference between equality and equality. In changing the way we think about the so-called educational and penal crises, we observed that equality serves to divert the attention of masses from the privileged position of a few. Demanding equality is in many ways acknowledging the higher position of a particular group and calling for changes that make other groups more like "them." It is in the end a plea for assimilation.

Litter (2013) unpacks "the marketing of equality under neoliberalism" in her work on "meritocracy as plutocracy" (p. 52). Litter (2013) defines meritocracy as the "the idea that whatever our social position at birth, society ought to offer enough opportunity and mobility for 'talent' to combine with 'effort' in order to rise to the top" (p. 52). The origins of the marketing equality in the United States originated in the early 1900s with the idea of what Litter (2013) calls aspirational consumerism emerged and defined the so-called American Dream.

The normalization of meritocracy is problematic for Litter (2013). It assumes that talent and intelligence are innate, endorses of systematic way of ranking people in which some people are by definition left behind, and "certain professions positioned at the top, by why they are there—and whether they should be there-tends to be less discussed" (p. 54). Another important problems Litter (2013) identifies is that meritocracy "functions as an ideological myth to obscure economic and social inequalities and the role it plays in curtailing social inequality" (p. 55).

Equity, on the other hand, "is the only potential course of action that could counterbalance the racist underpinnings of both educational and correctional structures" (Fasching-Varner et al. 2014, p. 424). Equity focuses society to confront the unequal treatment experienced by people of color and

people of low socioeconomic status and the lingering effects of that treatment on those populations today and in the foreseeable future.

The concept of educational and penal realism explains why racial disparities exist and persist in education and in the criminal justice system. The
concept also provides a way of explaining the ebbs and flows and cycles of
progression and recession. It explains the frustration and jubilance indigenous leader felt throughout history and provide clear and convincing evidence of the need to confront "oppression day by day and step by step in an
unapologetic way" (Fasching-Varner et al. 2014, p. 425) for "the fight itself
has meaning and should give us hope for the future" (Bell 1982, p. 378).

Whether or not the United States is a democracy or a plutocracy will
continue to be debated by scholars and others. What is clear is that the gap
between capitalist and workers is greater than every more and the gap is
likely to widen or remain the same over the foreseeable future. What is also
clear is that even if the United States is not a plutocracy, as some have
claimed, it surely possesses characteristics of one. The wealth control much
of the media, have a heavy hand in elections, and exert at least some control
of the legislative and fiscal processes in America. The control of the media
has led to a decline in important mediums of community engagement for
historically and economically disadvantaged groups, like blacks. It has lead
to representations of blackness that belong in the Ferris University Racist
Memorabilia Museum, the disenfranchisement of voters, and increased apathy about the merits of participatory governance. With no true choice in some
areas voters cast a ballot with their silence and what has happened is that you
have more and more places in the United States with largely minority populations and majority white governance.

Moreover, this chapter has shown that charity can come with a heavy
price tag. Philantrocapitalism is in many ways an illusion of humanitarianism
and altruism. The purpose for giving is not always for the common good, but
for one's own good. What we are seeing are capitalist pushers who create a
need for a poisonous product and then feed the poison to the people and then
give out turkeys at Thanksgiving and feel good that they are "giving back" or
making a difference. The poisons come in the form of social policies, which
attempt to capitalize on the misery of people of color such as educational
reform while appearing to address a critical social need. Doling out millions
of dollars to causes like educational reform may make plutocrats "feel good,"
but they do the public "little good."

Debates about President Obama's role as a key supporter of plutocrats
will likely be debated long after he completes his two terms in office. What is
interesting is the lack of visceral and vocal critiques of self-proclaimed plutocrats and plutocrats lurking in the shadows of the American social structure.
The impact of plutocrats on American society is significant and dispropor-

tionately impacts blacks who are one of the most marginalized groups in this country; whites, even poor whites, have at least middling authority.

The influence of wealth on governance has impacted the effectiveness of black leadership. It has made it increasingly difficult to be masters of change. The concentration of wealth and power continues to provide fertile soil for plutocrats to plant harmful public policy seeds which blossom into such things as poor educational reform that ensures that blacks and other people of color are the predominate group in the segment of necessary inequality in a functioning capitalist democracy.

Confronting plutocratic reign will require today what it has required in the past, "grass-roots activism, public protests, and demonstrations, and eventually bold leaders, indeed drawn from the rich but with their hearts with the people: Teddy Roosevelt, Franklin Roosevelt, and John F. Kennedy. Yet in all of these cases, the mass public led and the great leaders followed the case" (Sachs 2014). In the next chapter, we examine efforts to combat plutocratic reign as it relates to race and public education in America.

Chapter Eight

Fighting Back: Changing Trajectory of Public Education in America

Confronting seemingly insurmountable odds is nothing new to blacks in America or to other historically disadvantaged groups. However, the issues facing public education, especially the Wal-Martization of public schools, presents a unique set of challenges, the likes of which we have not seen in quite some time. Nevertheless, there are efforts underway to fight back and change the trajectory of public education in America. The chapter begins with the various ways blacks and others minority groups have resisted public policies and private actions that disproportionately impacted communities of color and undermined what we claim to value as a society. Next, a discussion of some of the dominant theories explaining why particular strategies are selected and the degrees to which they are successful follows. Then, case studies are presented involving grassroots community-based organizations, current and retired teachers, parent groups, and a university-community partnership, which illustrate the key characteristics that must be present in resistant efforts in order to reduce the risk of harm to black communities and to the broader society.

LET RESISTANCE BE YOUR MOTTO

Free blacks fought against the dominant racial ideology of the day in the decades leading up to the start of the Civil War. Gayle (1998) says resistance efforts were motivated by three key factors: "the material circumstances of black existence; Northern Black institutional formation undergirding emerging indigenous leadership and protest direction; and the overt and covert operations of vigilantism, dramatic slave rescues, and the Underground Railroad, all of which operated in tandem to each other" (p. 764).

Additionally, Gayle (1998) cites work on defense mobilization to explain how blacks respond to their political marginalization. Defense mobilization relies upon collection action and understanding which in turn plant the seeds for social change. "In the antebellum era, community consciousness fostered the connective tissue between early institutional formation and emerging leadership" (Gayle 1998, p. 764). The three variables Gayle (1998) described "provided the critical political support and agitation in Black communities as they defensively mobilized around two objectives of slave abolition and freedom and equality for free African Americans" (p. 764).

Gayle (1998) adds that protests are intended to shake things up-to challenge the status quo and to mobilize blacks toward collective action in an effort to produce transformative social change. Political activists may have led the way, but it was the "critical mass of support" that made change possible (p. 765). Outside support may come and go, but internal and organized rage and pain converted into persistent agitation and protest was much more of a threat to the status quo. "By attempting to force a disruption in political institutional arrangements to facilitate change, sustained political protest represents both a real and symbolic quest for political liberation" (Gayle 1998, p. 765).

Gayle (1998) cites the key roles the black church, mutual aid societies, and the black press played "to spearhead moral uplift and protest activity" (p. 770). The black church provided the spiritual support and mutual aid societies provided secular support, but taken together they were responsible for "heightening the community consciousness around the component of racial unity as a solidifying force and a transformative vehicle for political empowerment" (p. 770).

More specifically, Gayle (1998) makes the argument that the leadership role of the black church in resistance efforts began in the late 1700s with protests by Richard Allen and Absalom Jones when they left the Methodist Church in protest over the unequal treatment blacks received. Blacks followed Allen and Jones in large numbers and "their collective protest was the political spark that led to the founding of The Free African Society, a secular organization, and ultimately, the independent black church movement" (Gayle 1998, p. 771). The grassroots protests affirmed the leadership role of black clergy and endorsed protest as a mechanism for communicating dissatisfaction with an unjust system.

Gayle (1998) attributes some of the growth in size and influence of the black church to the role of mutual aid societies and fraternities as generators of black community economic development. Mutual aid societies not only had large memberships, but they also had access to a considerable amount of financial capital. These organizations served as "an economic support system in the community, these organizations provided assistance in the form of disability insurance, senior citizen allotment, and pensions to widows with dependent children" (p. 776). Moreover, mutual benefit societies also "operated schools for orphans as well as craft apprenticeship programs for black youth" (p. 776). They also were able to provide loans to black business owners.

The black press "collectively solidified the African American political voice into a critical mass" (Gayle 1998, p. 777). While church leaders in the mid-1800s could reach those in their congregations, the black press reached church members and those outside of the church. The black press could provide a way to debunk the myths that were so prevalent in the white press and show that blacks were invested and engaged in their own liberation. Gayle (1998) concludes, "resistance was inextricably tied to the institutional formation and emerging leadership in black communities. It was the community's sanction of these developmental processes as well as their financial support of these institutions and organizations that enabled their development.

Blacks continue to resist their marginalized position in society by creating opportunities for social inactions with other blacks despite the diminishing effectiveness of indigenous institutions due to the influence of wealth and the belief held by many that class matters more than race. Lewis and McKissic's (2010) work on black students on predominately white institutions provides a good example. The black community serves (for many) "as a dynamic and contested space where, despite what many students characterized as 'drama' among Black students, participants found support, grounding, and strength" (p. 265). Unlike earlier studies on the black community in the undergraduate experience, Lewis and McKissic (2010) "investigated the black community as an explanatory tool for resilience" (p. 265).

The black community serves as a source of resistance. The black community "facilitates African American students' execution of resistance practices—critical resistant navigational skills and oppositional behaviors" (Lewis and McKissic 2010, p. 266). Lewis and McKissic (2010) described critical resistant navigational skills as the ability to create relationships with other members of one's own racial group.

Participation in race-specific groups for blacks at predominately white institution leads to enhanced "knowledge and skills to resist the debilitating effects of racism present in the daily life of a college student of African descent" (Lewis and McKissic 2010, p. 266). Resistance practices maintain cultural integrity and extend the historic struggle for justice as well as challenges and transforms whitespace.

Lewis and McKissic (2010) described oppositional behaviors are described by as "actions that interrogate racist expressions and exhibitions and so lead to positive and meaningful change" (p. 266). For black students at majority white colleges and universities oppositional behaviors often lead to departure from the institution of higher learning prior to graduation. "Mass collective actions, such as protest rallies and sit-ins" are some examples of oppositional behaviors (p. 267).

el-Khoury (2012) focused on the black body in her work on resistance and management of self, which highlights the fact that resistance need not take place within an institution, but may be evidenced in the individual. Reflecting on the practice of racial profiling, el-Khoury (2012) describes the targeting of individuals on based upon shared physical characteristics as "a complex oppressive regime of racial dressage intended to discipline the black body that is co-extant with resistance to the state power and the matrix of domination" (p.85). This new regime creates new forms of resistance. The new forms of resistance are based upon a refuse to accept a subordinate status and reject the doctrine of white superiority.

"The spirit of resistance in the United States is principally against corporate capitalism and the white logic embedded in the system" (el-Khoury 2012, p.87) as well as social control from agencies with legitimate authority, such as the police. Efforts to reject the dehumanization and criminalization of black bodies are part of the everyday lived experiences of blacks in America. Blacks not only engage in this cultural maneuvering, but they also change power domains, argues, el-Khoury (2012).

el-Khoury (2012) draws from the literature on the "techniques of self" and applies them to racial dressage to show how blacks "revolutionize the self" (p. 89) and identifies a set of techniques and practices used to engineer one's inner self. The techniques and practices include: disposition of steadiness, rejecting criminalizing identities, discursive consciousness of the lesson, rejecting spatial power, and exhibiting disbelief in the system.

SOCIAL MOVEMENTS

Efforts to resist the contradictions and challenges associated with living in racialized social system may occur at all levels of society as evidenced in the roles of institutions and individuals. Collective efforts to address oppression are best understood through the various perspectives and lenses associated with the literature on social movements. Sociologists define social movements as collective efforts to bring about promote or resist changes in society. Social movements are typically coordinated, sustained, and occur outside of the expected norms or routines of society.

Social movements typically include goal setting. Goals within a movement may be clear or they may be hard to decipher. Individuals with the group may disagree on the specific goals of the movement as well as the best strategies for moving forward.

Individuals engaged in social movements may be represented by what scholars call social movement organizations. The mission, purpose, and goals of the organizations are within the spirit of the identified goals of the social movement. Sociologists have long been interested in understanding social movements and a number of theories and perspectives were developed over time including, collective behavior, mass society, and deprivation. We will now focus our attention on three of the more recent theories and perspectives on social movements, which include: resource mobilization, political process, and new social movements.

Political Process Theory

Political process theory (PPT) describes social movement mobilization and emphasizes "the role of political opportunities, mobilizing structures, and framing processes, along with protest cycles and contentious repertoires" (Caren 2007, p. 1). The theory rose in popularity in the 1970s and the 1980s and was based largely on efforts to analyze the civil rights movement. According to Caren (2007), political process theory focuses on the relationships between various movement attributes, including the ways in which organizations are structured and the broader contexts in which social movements occur. "Recent research by core PPT theorists has shifted focus to a more dynamic analysis of the reoccurring mechanisms and processes of contentious politics" (p. 1).

Amernta et al. (2010) wrote about political process theories and focused on the influences of social movements on policymaking. Influence on democratic rights, electoral processes, court decisions, state and local bureaucracies, and political parties should be the measures of success. The researchers defined political social movements as movements involving actors and organizations working toward changing the balance of power and to transform society through the state by mobilizing ordinary citizens for continuous political action. Political action may take many forms including: protests, marches, civil disobedience, lobbying, lawsuits, letters to the editor, and press conferences. Amernta et al. (2010) say the social movements that attracted the most attention over the past several decades included movements centered on issues of labor, African Americans, civil rights, veterans, feminists, nativists, and environmentalists. In studying social movements in America scholars traditionally ignore the impact of organizations external to the social movement organizations, specifically, those with decision-making authority, such as: political executives, legislators, and judges, and instead focus on success as defined by acceptance or new advantages. The authors conclude that movement protests are influential in setting policy agendas, but that there must be a move beyond that to address structural changes, such as winning demographic rights and transforming policies.

McCarthy and Zald (1977) first articulated resource mobilization theory almost forty years ago. The authors examined: the variety and sources of resources utilized by collective actors; the relationship between collective actors, media, authorities, and others; and the interaction among organizations. Resource mobilization theory also placed a great emphasis on the types of societal support and constraint collective actors receive. Prior to the introduction of resource mobilization theory the literature on social movements, according to McCarthy and Zald (1977), focused on shared grievances and generalized beliefs about the causes and ways of addressing grievances are important preconditions for social movements. The authors disagreed with the early literature on social movements and the underlying assumption that there was a close link between preexisting discontent and generalized belief in the rise of social movements. Additionally, McCarthy and Zald (1977) find that too much emphasis is placed on the psychology of collective actions and which persons devote not enough attention to the process and institutions external to the collectivity become involved in social movements.

Other important differences between resource mobilization theory and previous theories about social movements were outlined in the classic work by McCarthy and Zald (1977). Concerning the support bases, traditional theories say social movements are based upon populations with concern that provides the labor and resources necessary to bring about change. Resource mobilization theory, on the other hand, contends "social movements may or may not be based upon the grievances of the presumed beneficiaries" (p. 1216). In fact, some supporters may provide a variety of resources and have "no commitment to the values that underlie specific movements" (p. 1216).

McCarthy and Zald (1977) further argue that in traditional theories on social movements leaders use one of three strategies to bring about change: bargaining, persuasion, or violence. Conversely, resource mobilization theory holds that the social movement organizations have other options, including: "mobilizing supporters, neutralizing and/or transforming mass and elite publics into sympathizers, achieving change in targets" and "tactics are influenced by interorganizational competition and cooperation" (p. 1217).

Finally, it can be said that traditional approaches to understanding social movements focus on case studies and ignore the roles of external forces in shaping the movement organizations goals and purposes. With resource mobilization theory, there is an understanding that "society provides the infrastructure which social movement industries and other industries utilize. The aspects utilized include communication media and expense, levels of affluence, degree of access to institutional centers, preexisting networks, and occupational structure and growth" (p. 1217).

The scholarly work on collective identities and social movements are useful here. Efforts to resist contemporary educational reforms are centered on a sense of shared identity, often based upon race, occupation, or other social status. Polletta and Jasper (2001) provide a nice summary of much of the literature on collective identity and social movements. Collective identity addressed issues not adequately addressed in political process and research mobilization theories on social movements. According to Polletta and Jasper (2001), individuals engaged in resistance efforts were viewed as "irrational individuals propelled into protest by crowd contagion or system strain (p. 283). Research mobilization and political process theories addressed access to resources required for engagement in resistance activities. "But their emphasis on the how mobilization over the why of it, their focus on the state as target of action, and their dependence on rationalist images of individual action left important issues unexamined" (p. 283).

Collective identities theories address four key problems to address the gaps in the literature. First collective identity examines why collectives come together when then do. Second, the literature on collective identity also examines what moves people to act. "Collective identity seemed to capture better the pleasures and obligations that actually persuade people to mobilize. Identity was appealing, then, as an alternative to material incentives" (p. 284).

Polletta and Jasper (2001) also say the collective identity literature addresses a shortcoming of the literature on social movements as it relates to strategic choices. "If people choose to participate because doing so accords with who they are, the forms of protest they choose are also influenced by collective identities" (p. 284).

Lastly, conventional approaches to understanding social movements have focused more on outcomes than on the culture. "Movements also transform cultural representations, social norms—how groups see themselves and are seen by others. Changes in collective identity captured movement impacts beyond institutional reform" (Polletta and Jasper 2001, p. 284).

New social movement scholars challenged the idea that collective interests are sustained over relatively long periods of time. New social movement theorists contend that it is not class position, for example that accounts for participation in social movements but collective actors "sought recognition for new identities and lifestyles" (Polletta and Jasper 2001, p. 286).

The significance of collective identities has increased over time, claim Polletta and Jasper (2001). During the historic civil rights and labor movements integration, equality, and inclusion were the main goals, whereas, in the post-rights era collective actors have more flexibility in defining and constructing their own identities. Drawing from the literature in network analysis, Polletta and Jasper (2001) also made the claim that the identities of collective actors are no longer fixed categories, such as in the cases of race, class, and gender; rather, collective actors share "common positions in networks," such as urban living, political affiliation (p. 298). Polletta and Jasper (2001) conclude, collective actors "may engage in moral protest to develop the kind of self we want; that what is considered a good strategy is often based on what groups it is symbolically associated with; and that movements provide new identities as a way to gain power as well as transform selves" (p. 298–299).

Buras (2011) highlights key principles in guiding the reform of public schools throughout the country. The principles are based upon limitations in conventional theories and perspectives on social movements, particularly those which do not measure success by public policy transformation, do not involve grassroots individuals and groups, fail to account for the roles of external social movement organizations, and examine social movements from either a micro- or a macro-level vantage point.

According to Buras (2011), the reform of public schools must be neighborhood-based; exclude barriers to enrollment and retention; respectful of the contributions, rights, and benefits of veteran teachers; prepared to recognize teacher unions; welcome substantive and democratic participation of grassroots communities in educational decision making; and reflect governmental transparency and accountability (p. 323–324). The case studies that follow are rooted in the core principles outlined by Buras (2011), which must be in place to address public education in America in a way that is grassroots and community- and student-centered.

In Baton Rouge, Louisiana, MetroMorphosis is leading an initiative to improve local public schools in a manner that is "neighborhood-based," "welcoming of substantive and democratic participation of grassroots communities, and transparency and accountability in the allocation and use of public monies based on legitimate, sustained, and widespread community input" (Buras 2011, p. 324).

MetroMorphosis was established in 2012 to lead inner city residents in the design and implementation of solutions to enduring neighborhood problems. The challenges facing residents in Baton Rouge, especially in North Baton Rouge where much of the organizations educational reform efforts are directed, are many. The organization's official website cites the following conditions,

> Baton Rouge has struggled with the entrenched and interrelated issues of economic disparities, struggling schools and poor health outcomes, all within the current context of the nation's severe economic turmoil. The inner-city is plagued with economic disparities magnified by a high poverty rate which is three percentage points above the national average (17.2 percent vs. 14.3 percent), and by nearly one in four children living below the poverty line. Graduation rates in East Baton Rouge Parish schools continue to decline along with other challenges that include truancy, achievement gaps, the retention of qualified teachers and community involvement.

To combat the issues facing inner-city neighborhoods in Baton Rouge, the "MetroMorphosis Model" seeks to lead residents in embarking on "a journey to re-invent a city. Strategically convening and catalyzing both community leaders and residents" to the creation of "new approaches, strengthening social networks and moving communities forward to implement lasting change."

Clearly, education is a focal point of the organization's mission as is an understanding of how complex the issues are facing city residents, particularly those in North Baton Rouge. Led by Reverend Raymond Jetson, the organization consists of several core programs: Urban Congregations Initiative, Better Baton Rouge, Urban Leadership Development Initiative, and Our Schools Our Excellence.

Urban Congregations area of focus is on building the capacity of faith-based institutions to meet the challenges facing residents in Baton Rouge, especially residents living in North Baton Rouge. This includes enhancing the ability of those in the faith community to assess, mobilize, and engage congregants. It also involves assisting urban congregations in measuring success and impact. While the black church has played a historic role in the African American experience, the ability of the black church to address issues facing black communities, particularly with respect to education, may be hindered by the influence of wealth elites and the intentional (and unintentional) ways in which their power and influence has limited the effective of black churches as discussed in the previous chapter. MetroMorphosis hopes that their work with create an environment whereby "for the first times since perhaps the Civil Rights Movement, the robust capacity of urban congregations will be present and accounted for in leading positive change."

Kanter et al. (2014) describe Better Baton Rouge as the impetus behind the formation of MetroMorphosis. The Harvard Business School scholars described the creation of a community-board soon after Jetson's return from participating in Harvard's prestigious Advanced Leadership Institute, which later became known as Better Baton Rouge. The purpose of the group was to "think about precisely what form a container for future 'citizen-led' action in Baton Rouge should take" (p. 13). Better Baton Rouge relies upon innovation clusters or "small groups of community leaders organized around a shared passion." The three clusters focus on access to health food options, youth development, and education. The healthy food cluster is responsible for planning community gardens at local schools and for bringing farmers markets with limited access to fresh and nutritious food. The youth cluster works to enhance leadership skills and provide opportunities for young people to serve their respective communities.

Urban Leadership Development Initiative provides training for emerging leaders in the MetroMorphosis's targeted communities. Participants are taught "how to identify opportunities, develop innovative solutions, and to build collations to implement innovative solutions." The program is based upon the principles of adaptive and advanced leadership, which involves participants engaging "in a rigorous curriculum designed to equip, position, and challenge them to act as a catalytic agent of change." Participants receive the added benefit of being mentored by Rev. Raymond Jetson and other community leaders to prepare them "to accept new challenges in order to make a greater societal impact."

Our Schools Our Excellence is working to improve the quality of the schools in North Baton Rouge. Rev. Jetson convened a series of community conversations around the issue of public school education. A set of mandates were agreed upon and "identified as essential to initiating authentic positive change in North Baton Rouge K–12 public schools. The mandates include: a focus on student success and the recruitment, reward, and empowerment of principals and teachers through schools in North Baton Rouge. Moreover, Our Schools Our Excellence also calls for greater involvement of parents and for "schools and community partners to provide academic, behavioral, and social support to both students and their families."

MetroMorphosis recruited community members to serve the community as an "advocate in excellence" and join "in fighting for excellence." Residents were asked to take inventory of their skills and commitment before literally signing-up to meet the challenges facing public schools in North Baton Rouge. MetroMorphosis identifies the qualities of an advocate as:

- Learner—Continually seeking to learn more about education issues in our community.
- Listener—Hears what others are saying and respects the opinions of others.
- Communicator—Can clearly and persuasively share the importance of excellent schools for our children.
- Determined—The advocate is firmly committed to every child having access to an excellent school.
- Trustworthy—The advocate values the need for being credible and honest to everyone involved.
- Focused—The advocate is passionate about Our Schools Our Excellence while speaking to others and promotion action.

Advocates work toward the mission of fostering "an environment that creates excellent educational and life outcomes for children attending school in North Baton Rouge" in four working groups: communications, community involvement, parental engagement, and youth involvement. The purpose of the community involvement group is to increase the number of community participants engaged in Our Schools Our Excellence. The community involvement group identified a number of events advocates could attend in an effort to garner support for Our Schools Our Excellence, including youth sporting events, community health fairs, and community meal programs, and holiday gatherings for the community.

The communications group shares "the initiatives and strategies of Our Schools Our Excellence with the goal of sustaining and increasing active community, parental and youth engagement and support. Recently, the communications group decided to focus on outreach to faith-based organizations, school alumni groups, youth sports leagues, and local business owners, with a particular focus on stylist and barber shops—places young people visit regularly and with whom young people may have strong ties. Longer-term goals included training advocates, hosting events to engage the community, and use various platforms to increase access to meetings, including live-streaming of meetings.

The parental engagement group "aggressively seeks to continually increase the participation of parents and caregivers in Our School and Our Excellence and are actively committed to excellent educational and life outcomes." This group agreed to survey parents and create relevant parent groups and workshops. Additionally, the parental engagement group decided to "connect with Head Start Program to generate involvement, select neighborhoods to canvass and disseminate information, and connect with civic centers and community groups to build parent participation."

The youth involvement group of the Our Schools Our Excellence initiative "works to continually increase the participation of students from North Baton Rouge schools in Our Schools Our Excellence. This group, largely comprised of youth, serves as a voice for students across the area." The group also decided to undertake a survey. The group would disseminate the survey to youth in North Baton Rouge and work to create new partnerships between various community organizations focused on youth.

MetroMorphosis appears well on its way towards mobilizing residents in North Baton Rouge to address the educational issues facing students and the structure reflects many of the core principles outlined. An articulation of efforts to specifically effectuate public policy changes would assist with making the desired changes sustainable and transformative.

In Buffalo, New York, there is a university-community partnership underway aimed at addressing issues facing public schools in a city long described as one of the most segregated cities in the nation. Dr. Henry Louis Taylor and Linda McGlynn outlined the model behind Futures Academy in a recent paper about what they describe as the community as classroom initiative. The University at Buffalo, State University of New York, Center for Urban Studies, is engaged in efforts "to build a university-assisted community school centered neighborhood development initiative in the Fruit Belt, a distressed community in Buffalo, New York. The goal is to turn Futures Academy (School 37), a traditional Pre-K through eighth grade public school into a university-assisted community school that drives the neighborhood regeneration process in the Fruit Belt," (Taylor and McGlynn 2010, p. 32) a historic neighborhood in the City of Buffalo. The concept of a university-assisted community school is rooted in the idea that a university-assisted community school "is both a place and set of partnerships and activities that turn a traditional school into a 'hub' for the community and an entity that helps to education, engage, empower and serve all members of the community in which the school is located" (Taylor and McGlynn 2010, p. 32). The school serves as an anchor institution, as Franklin argues, has been the historical function of schools in black communities, at least. Connecting the school and the community means that residents will see "the school as a neighborhood institution that should be preserved and developed" (Taylor and McGlynn 2010, p. 32).

The second important idea underpinning the concept of a university-assisted community school is that the sets of partnerships established as a result of connecting the academics, community-based activities, neighborhood development, and social services become one collaborative working toward a goal of transforming the distressed neighborhood in which it is located. With this context, the school becomes "the central hub around which neighborhood life evolves, community schools are strategically positioned to lead the regeneration process" (Taylor and McGlynn 2010, p. 32). The school does not replace historic institutions, but serves as a way to ensure that indigenous institutions remain connected and works together to create economically autonomous and sustainable communities that withstand internal and external threats, including the privatization of public schools and the general tendency of those with high levels of wealth, status, and power, to capitalize on the misery of subordinate groups.

Taylor and McGlynn (2010) contend that efforts to reform and transform schools cannot exist independent of efforts to revitalize and transform distressed neighborhoods. Underperforming schools and distressed neighborhoods are essentially two sides of the same coin and thus "must be solved conjointly" (Taylor and McGlynn 2010, p. 32). The authors further argue that schools can be a catalyst for neighborhood change and the site of collaboration where "authentic struggles to transform their community" can take place (Taylor and McGlynn 2010, p. 32). The role of the university is to leverage the institutions human and fiscal resources to support community schools.

Transforming a traditional school into a community school is not an easy task. Described as "an extremely complex process," Taylor and McGlynn (2010) say there are three critical elements:

1. Developing an action-oriented, problem-based pedagogical model that enables students to apply the knowledge learned inside the academic classroom to solve real-world neighborhood problems outside the

school building, along with popularizing the academic based community service learning courses within the university;

2. Transforming the school into a hub of neighborhood life and culture and a laboratory of democracy where parents, teachers, students, and residents and stakeholders work collaboratively to build the neighborhood and enhance the school;

3. Turning the community into an environment where residents and stakeholders are engage in lifelong learning, are highly supportive of academic achievement, and are engaged in the quest to improve the school; a learning community (Taylor and McGlynn 2010, p. 33).

The pedagogical approach involves challenging the way people in the community think about education. "Education is typically advertised as a ticket out of the neighborhood, a way to achieve the good life; it is a form of individual advancement that eschews group loyalty. Education is meant to be individually and personally rewarding, not communally transformative" (Taylor and McGlynn 2010, p. 34).

There are four components of the community to classroom initiative: neighborhood-building, community heritage, community parks and gardens, and community art. The neighborhood-building component enhances the ability of students to make the connections between "public policy and the city and neighborhood development process" (Taylor and McGlynn 2010, p. 37). The community heritage component creates pride and a collective identity for neighborhood residents by imparting the history of the Fruit Belt neighborhood, "its process of development, and forces that have driven its development over time" (Taylor and McGlynn 2010, p. 38). Students involved in the initiative kicked-off a research project where they laid the groundwork for the social history of houses in the Fruit Belt neighborhood. The social history of neighborhood houses will be used to develop a housing preservation plan.

Taylor and McGlynn (2010) described both the community parks and gardens and community art projects components of the community as classroom initiative in their article. The authors describe the community parks and gardens as "the most important neighborhood place making activities" in the initiative (p. 39) for it brings the community "together to turn unkempt vacant lots into parks, vegetable gardens, playgrounds, and recreational areas" (p. 39). While the community art project show students from inner city neighborhoods "how they can change the way their neighborhood looks and feels" (p.39). The students engage in activities where they re-imagine what their cities could and should look like.

Another example of an organized effort to resist current trends in American public schools can be found in the group, Badass Teachers Association (BATs). The association has local organizations in every state and boasts tens of thousands of supporters. Mark Naison, professor of African American Studies and history at Fordham University, is one of the founders. According to the group's official website, the mission is "to give voice to every teacher who refuses to be blamed for the failure of our society to erase poverty and inequality through education. BATs members refuse to accept assessments, tests and evaluations created and imposed by corporate driven entities that have contempt for authentic teaching and learning."

Naison (2013) described in a TED Talk, the transcripts of which are posted online, how he became an advocate for teachers and for public education. He described the joys of working with teachers and students in schools throughout the Bronx, New York, as part of the Bronx African American Historical Project. The project was established to address gaps in the literature on blacks in New York City in general, and blacks in the Bronx, in particular. Naison was regularly invited to local schools to share his research findings and to train teachers so they could develop local history projects in their schools. The local history projects provided students with a positive self-image and a sense of pride in their neighborhoods—neighborhoods that historically were portrayed in the media as the poster child for poverty, violence, criminal behavior, and generational despair.

At the height of Naison's work with students and teachers in the Bronx, a shift in the nation's largest school district occurred. The rating system for New York City Public Schools were established and the ratings for individual schools were published, which was a form of public shaming not only for the schools themselves, but also for the students, teachers, administrators, and families connected to the respective schools, especially schools deemed failing. After witnessing the firing of teachers en masse and the psychological toll the rating system and high stakes testing placed on all involved, Naison said he could not remain silent about what he witnessed and soon learned that what he was seeing was not unique to the Bronx, or to New York City, or the suburban schools on Long Island he visited, rather these were issues facing students, teachers, and families across the nation.

BATs has taken an official stand on a host of educational policy issues, including Common Core, informing parents, teachers, students, and activities with information to support them in their efforts to bend the arc of current educational policies toward the people most impacted, most invested, most at-risk, and with the most to lose. For example, BATs issued an official statement on Common Core aimed at demythologizing several ideas promoted by educational reformers (10 Things BATs Know about Common Core 2013). For example, the goal of common core is to make all students college and career ready. The group argues there is no research linking Common Core to college and career readiness. Moreover, BATs says "all children are not or will not be college and career ready for many different reasons." BATs also challenge that claim that Common Core will make American students more competitive with students in the world's top-performing countries. On the contrary, BATs says Common Core State Standards "were not benchmarked against other countries' standards" and that other countries "don't place much, if any, emphasis on testing." Furthermore, BATs say CCSS "tests are nothing more than the precursor for national standardized testing. They are culturally biased, incapable of measuring non-verbal learning or complex thought, and will ultimately cost more than they're worth."

BATs, like other entities comprised of diverse populations fighting towards a set of common goals, has experienced some inner conflict. While all BATs want to reduce or eliminate the use of high stakes testing, preserve academic freedom in the classroom, and include input from teachers, students, and parents in policy decisions affecting students, there are disagreements about how to achieve these goals and the extent to which issues such as race and racism are factors. Consequently, BATs has created a number of working groups, online and in the "real world" to focus specifically on the roles of race and racism, not only with respect to current educational policies, but even with the larger association of activists teachers who make up BATs.

Based upon the criteria developed for public school reform outlined by Buras (2011), along with Taylor and McGlynn's (2010) demonstration that school reform and neighborhood revitalization must be hand-in-hand, I created an index to evaluate the risk-levels to communities of color, especially to black communities. Any effort to change the current state of public education in America must be neighborhood-based; exclude barriers to enrollment and retention; respectful of the contributions, rights, and benefits of veteran teachers; prepared to recognize teacher unions; welcome substantive and democratic participation of grassroots communities in educational decision making; reflect governmental transparency and accountability; and also include an emphasis on neighborhood revitalization.

Educational reform efforts with zero components pose the greatest threat level to communities of color. Reform efforts with 1–2 components present a high risk, while reform efforts with 3–4 present a moderate risk. Efforts with 5 or more present a low-risk to communities of color. Educational reform driven by those adopting the Wal-Mart approach place communities of color at high risk because the efforts are not neighborhood based, seldom include communities in decision-making positions, vilify veteran teachers, seek to disrupt efforts to organization, establish restrictive admission and retention requirements, and ignore the need to address the host of issues facing distressed communities.

Some advocacy groups may unwittingly pose a threat to communities of color in the fight to redefine America's public schools if they are not careful. Advocacy groups that ignore too many of the key elements outlined here may end up doing more harm than good.

The threat to communities of color in the MetroMorphosis Model and the Futures Academy are low. The MetroMorphosis Model, which includes Our Schools Our Excellence, works to reinvent the North Baton Rouge in tandem with reinventing the educational experiences of the students living and learning within the surrounding neighborhood. Not only is the initiative neighborhood-based, as outlined previously, but Our Schools Our Excellence advocates access for all and engages in a host of demographic processes, which ensures that community members are not only involved in the decision-making process, but also insures that the quality of their participation is meaningful and moves beyond the tokenism that has been the signature of public participation in far too many cases. Moreover, MetroMorphosis supports and values teachers and trains community residents to advocate on behalf of children in North Baton Rouge, calling for accountability from all stakeholders and government officials.

Futures Academy is also representative of a low-risk approach to educational reform. The initiative is based upon the assumption that schools must serve as the central hub of a community and the transformation of distressed neighborhoods must include the simultaneous transformation of neighborhood schools. Leveraging the fiscal and human capital of the University at Buffalo means the community will enhance planning and implementation of essential programing in the community. Meetings between veteran teachers and university personnel reflect respect and support for the educators' expertise and the expertise of the university personnel. The emphasis on the connectedness between the community and the classroom and the level of community engagement further demonstrates the significance placed upon meaningful involvement and input from the community in mapping out the direction of public education and the broader community.

Likewise, Badass Teachers believes any efforts to change the way teaching and learning is done in American public schools must take into consideration the fact that schooling does not occur in a vacuum. Attention to the issues facing distressed communities must also be addressed and that solutions to challenges students and neighborhood face must come from the bottom-up. BATs also fights vehemently for teachers and their rights to organize. BATs demands decision-making authority be placed in the hands of teachers and families and not plutocrats. Adherence to each of these principles of reforms justifies placing the association of teachers at low-risk for harming communities most affected by the current trends in public education.

As in case where risk is assessed, risk levels can change. Any educational policy can cause more or less risk to communities of color than at previous times. Likewise, advocacy groups can change their focus and strategies and intentionally—or unwittingly—find themselves more in sync with out-of-touch reformers, than with the communities they claim to give voice to. It is imperative that educational policies, as well as resistance efforts, are continually revisited.

Education should not be a privilege, but a civil right. There is a social movement underway to address and eliminate the threat (and the harm) posed by educational reform policies that are being handed down by individuals with little or no educational background, but more importantly, with seemingly little or no regard for the harm inflicted on the millions of children of color for whom public schools are the only option. Dr. Henry Taylor (2005) described the main goal of the movement against the adoption of what I call the big box model to public education in an address back in 2005 sponsored by The Center for Community Partnerships, University of Pennsylvania.

Dr. Taylor (2005) described what he called the "Harriet Tubman" approach to education. He said, Tubman did not set out to dismantle slavery (p. 2). Tubman set out to free as many people as she could from the unjust institution. "In the Harriet Tubman approach to education the goal is to get people out of the ghetto and their responsibility is to go back and get someone else out" (p.2). Taylor went on to say that our goal should be poverty reduction and "the achievement of higher freedom" (p.2). Higher freedom means people should not only have the right to participate in a democratic process but also be free from schools designed to ensure their failure.

Just how successful the current movement will be remains to be seen. However, this chapter places the movement within the context of other American social movements and provides a mechanism for evaluating whether current and future educational policies pose a risk to historically disadvantaged groups, such as those living in urban areas, and people of color.

Chapter Nine

Worth the Fight

The privatization of American public schools is well on its way, particularly in communities of color. Non-blacks and income rich Americans are not totally immune. Even some non-blacks with middling authority are pushing back against movements toward standardized and high stakes testing that is taking a psychological toll on their children and uses arbitrary measures to assess their children's learning which goes counter to the relatively freedom and autonomy most have enjoyed. Although education reform is far-reaching, without question, communities of color are suffering the most and will continue to suffer if the current state of affairs is not challenged. In this book I have laid out just why and how the application of business models, such as the big box store model, is negatively affecting black communities in particular, and will continue to do so into the foreseeable future.

In a so-called post-racial society it is a challenge for some to show how and in what ways race matters. With so many voices pointing to examples of racial progress and ethnic harmony, the voices of those sounding the alarm that not only does race still matter, but also racism is alive and well, must continue to ring out. Just as in the days of old, public policies and private practices were put into place to limit the ability of blacks to fully compete with their white counterparts in all areas of society, but especially in the labor market and limited access to education was one way to make sure that blacks would not be in competition for whites with jobs. Additionally, educational opportunities were not only withheld from blacks, but also used as a means of disenfranchising black voters. It was understood by blacks throughout history that the acquisition of knowledge could not only lead to a good paying job and asset ownership, but also it was understood that the acquisition of knowledge was a revolutionary act that would lead to a period of personal and collective enlightenment, which would empower the individual and the community at-large to always have the tools within to fight oppression from without. Thus, schools were and will always be grounds where sociopolitical contestation occurs.

While little has changed with respect to the creation of structures and institutions to place blacks in a lower position in society than whites, what has changed are the number and relative power and influence of America's super-rich. America has always been home to wealthy citizens who have used their power and influence to impact legislation, but the number of super-rich and the gap between the super-rich and everyone else has never been greater. Recent judicial decisions have also opened the floodgates for the super-rich to use their financial and social capital to influence elections there therefore change public policies in ways unimaginable decades ago. Corporate elites have successfully demonstrated their ability to exert their will even in the face of resistance.

There is an education growth machine at work that is more interested in maximizing profits than creating lifelong learners. Business owners, and some communities, are embracing a model with origins in Arkansas, which destroyed many small businesses in its wake, depressed wages, offered cheap goods made by competing countries, all the while selling the enterprise as one that would help people live better and save. By most accounts, the young people of today will not live better than their parents and few with have anything to save, but the plutocrats driving the public school systems in ditches of despair will continue to be enriched and will continue efforts to convince the public that they are doing is for the good of the public. The super-rich will continue attempts to convince the masses that because they are rich, they know what is best for those who are not. They will hold out the fantasy that if the masses would simply work hard they too could join the ranks of the super-rich. This book also made clear that the idea that we are living in a meritocracy is indeed a myth.

All hope is not lost. Despite the loss of indigenous organizations and educational leaders at the hands of non-educators with the resources to dominate others, a number of notable and replicable models for mobilizing students, parents, teachers, administrators, and entire communities in a collective movement to begin to transform public schools, communities, and public policies on local, state, and national levels are well on their way. What more can we do?

As part of an ongoing research effort to assess attitudes about American public schools, I solicited responses from individuals over the age of eighteen using social media. I posted a link to an online, confidential questionnaire for a period of thirty days. I posted the link to a number of Facebook Groups, including groups for educators, educators of colors, parents and teachers organized for and against the Common Core, and various parents association. I also submitted the link to selected educators and asked the educators to share the link with others. I received seventeen responses to the series of largely open-ended questions posed to the participants. The age range for the survey was 21–67. The majority of respondents were females and most were educators. Thirty-seven percent of respondents (6) were black, thirty-two percent of respondents were white (7). One respondent identified as Asian and one respondent identified as Hispanic. Another respondent identified as other. Using the educational levels of the respondents and the self-identified incomes, all of the respondents would be considered middle-class. The lowest level of education for participants was a Master's Degree.

All of the respondents expect one said public education is a civil right. The one person who did not see public education as a civil right said that public education is a civil rights issue, but not a civil right. Almost all of the respondents said the purpose of public schools was to provide a quality education for all. However, one respondent said the purpose of education is to create "good followers" and the public education is a "tool to dummy down independent thought, critical analysis and out of the box thinking. To spread entitlement and supremacy thinking for certain people and reinforce through history, science and literature the inferiority of some people in the world."

When asked to identify the top five issues affecting public education in America the responses echoed the core issues addressed through this book, including: unequal access, lack of resources, global competitiveness, for-profit charter schools, high stakes testing, unfunded mandates, racism, privatization, union busting, poverty, lack of support for teachers, and the creation of a crisis that can only be resolved through expensive testing.

I asked the respondents to reflect upon the legacy of education policies, specifically No Child Left Behind and respondents said NCLB shall forever be remembered for turning education into a business and for leaving behind an entire generation of students who were robbed of their opportunities, used as guinea pigs, and produced "the lost generation."

When asked what role the business community should play in public education responds said volunteering and mentoring were more appropriate roles for the business community than setting educational policies. Endowments and scholarships are some other ways the business community can support educators, students, and their families. Moreover, respondents said the business community could work with educators to ensure that the skills students acquire meet the needs of the business community.

Respondents were not only asked to comment on the role of the business community but also the roles of legislators, parents, and educators. Respondents want more financial support from their representatives and they want their elected officials to make decisions that reflect the needs of the community not the needs of corporate interests. One respondent went as far as to say that legislators should "require diversity on school boards, establish term limits for board members and superintendents, and establish a fair teacher evaluation process."

Educators should modernize pedagogical techniques. Educators must be open to seeing educational facilities as "primary sites of nutrition, social services, and civil training," and should therefore welcome trained professionals (e.g., human service providers) as partners. Educators must also work to shape educational policy and become culturally competent.

Respondents called upon parents to become more informed, concerned, and proactive—demanding state representatives pass laws that benefit students such as opting out of standardized tests. At the same time, respondents believe that no matter high parents set standards for their children that they are largely powerless in the political process.

While the findings are not generalizable the findings are informative and do provide some insight as to what a particular segment of population believes is required to change what some view as the undermining of local control and what one respondent referred to as a "collaboration of both political parties in efforts to privatize public schools and take over what goes on in classrooms away from teachers."

In addition to the suggestions proposed by respondents we must also address transportation issues in the long and short terms efforts to address the varying experiences of students and teachers in American public schools by race. Currently, there are students, largely students of color, waking up earlier than some enlisted soldiers waiting for buses that will take them miles away from their homes to school or to transportation hubs and then to school. The commuting time for some high school students is over ninety minutes and we are not talking about only in rural areas. Whether under the guise of integrating schools by busing students of one race to schools where that race is underrepresented or where students receive public transportation to magnet and charter schools somewhere in the student's general geographical location, there students who stand at bus stops as early as 5:00 am in some places to begin a long commute to school which likely begins shortly after 7:00 am. These students were then expected to excel academically throughout the day, including performing well on standardized tests and other assessment tools, only to make the two-hour reverse commute at the end of the day. Most adults would dread a four-hour per day commute to work and yet thousands of children of color are asked or forced to do just that.

There must also be an acknowledgement that education is important for individuals, families, communities, and for the society at-large for many reasons. However, we must debunk the myth that education is the key to success, that education is the key to upward mobility. There must be an acknowledgement that education as a social institution is one of the most effective at controlling selected populations, perpetuating inequality, and justifying the unequal treatment of racial and ethnic minority groups through the criminalization, demonization, stereotyping and misrepresentation of these communities.

Schools not only feed the prison pipeline, but also act as network theorists have argued in research on corporate governance, as networks of sub-structures of wealth, power, and status operate. Since schools serve such an important role in perpetuating inequality, it is counterintuitive for those most negatively affected to look for solutions from within traditional systems.

Parents should provide as much academic support to their parents as possible. Where parents are unable to provide such support, indigenous organizations must fill-in the gap. The black church, black fraternal organizations, and non-profit organizations serving largely minority populations must position themselves to provide academic support, mentoring, apprenticeship, business development, and financial literacy to all members of the community, including to students and their parents.

Community residents must demand that businesses where blacks spend their dollars return the favor by reinvesting in the community in ways that reflect true partnerships, this includes hiring people from within the community and giving them a living wage. It also involves mentoring the next generation of business owners and wealth builders so that the community is not perpetually dependent upon external funding but is self-sufficient.

The black community and those sympathizing with the historical struggle for social justice should never again equate integration with equity, equality, and excellence. What has happened as a result is the mistaken belief that as a society we have moved from a system where blacks were solidly on the bottom, to the establishment of a seemingly parallel system that was separate but equal back, to a system where blacks were again, solidly on the bottom. In actuality, the position of blacks in the social structure has never changed. Even in an overtly black and white world, blacks were at the bottom of the social structure and education played a critical role. In the preindustrial period blacks had little or no access to education. During the industrial period blacks had access to a segregated educational system, and in the post-industrial period blacks have access to a segregated educational system, which provides blacks with limited or no access to an education that members in dominant group enjoy. Resistance efforts must continue and must expand. The case studies highlighted provide a framework for developing strategies that are community-based and child-focused.

Schools must be seen as Taylor (2005) argued as anchors and not as anvils. Anchors in a nautical sense keep a vessel in place and prevent it from being dragged away in the event of a strong gust of wind, for example. In the world of sports, the anchor is the strongest person on relay team and in the world of business an anchor store is a prominently placed establishment that draws consumers and the expectation is that consumers will patronize the neighboring stores. Capitalist educational reformers seek to replace indigenous leaders and institutions with big box schools, but community members must continue to fight to ensure that schools become a focal part of the community, which invites members to participate and provide mutual support. Capitalist educational reforms see schools not as community anchors, but at anvils used to hammer out tools to be used to enhance their bottom line.

I have shown that the United States is not a post-racial society and persistent educational inequality is evidence of that fact. The adoption of the big box model to public education is one of the latest iterations of efforts to maintain the racial status quo in America, which is based upon the fallacy of the doctrine of white supremacy and black inferiority. There are no easy answers. It is not going to be easy to match the power and influence of educational entrepreneurs also known as plutocrats, also known as philanthrocapitalists, also known as educational reformers; but we owe it to our children, to our nation, and to ourselves to keep trying.

References

10 Things BATs Know about Common Core. November 13, 2013. Retrieved from http://withabrooklynaccent.blogspot.com/2013/11/10-things-bats-know-about-common-core.html. on November 22, 2014.

Adams, Harry. "Against Plutocracies: Fighting Political Corruption." *Constellations* 15, no. 1 (2008): 126–147.

Adams, Ronald. "David v. Goliath: A Brief Assessment of the U.S. Supreme Court's 2011 Ruling Denying Class Certification in *Dukes v Wal-Mart.*" *Business and Society Review* 118, no. 2 (2013): 253–270.

Alexander, Michelle. *The New Jim Crow: Mass Incarceration in the Age of Colorblindness.* New York: The New Press, 2012.

Amenta, Edwin, Caren, Neal, Chiarello, Elizabeth, and Su Yang. "The Political Consequences of Social Movements." *Annual Review of Sociology* 36 (2010): 287–307.

Amistad Collection at Tulane University. "School Desegregation in Louisiana." *Encyclopedia of Louisiana History, Culture and Community.* Louisiana Endowment for the Humanities, n.d. Web. Mar. 2014.

Arcia, Emily. "Variability in School's Suspension Rates of Black Students." *The Journal of Negro Education* 76, no. 4 (2007): 597–608.

Arnold, Regina. "Processes of Victimization and Criminalization of Black Women." *Social Justice* 17, no. 3 (1990): 153–166.

Arnstein, Sherry. "A Ladder of Citizen Participation." *Journal of American Institute of Planners* 35 (1969): 216–224.

Asimakopoulos, Jeffrey. "The Civil Rights-Black Power Era, Direct Action, and Defensive Violence: Lessons for the Working-Class Today." *Theory in Action* 3, no. 1 (2010): 42.

Austin, James, Clear, Todd, Duster, Troy, Greenberg, David, Irwin, John, McCoy, Candace, Mobley, Alan, Owen, Barbara, and Joshua Page. (2007). *Unlocking America: Why and How to Reduce America's Prison Population.* Washington, DC: JFA Institute.

Bankston, Carl L. and Stephen J. Caldas. *A Troubled Dream: The Promise and Failure of School Desegregation in Louisiana.* Nashville: Vanderbilt UP, 2002.

Bankston, Carl L. and Stephen J. Caldas. "Family structure, schoolmates, and the racial inequalities in school achievement." *Journal of Marriage and the Family 60*, no. 3 (1998): 715–723.

Barkan, Joanne. "Plutocrats at Work: How Big Philanthropy Undermines Democracy." *Social Research* 80, no.2 (2013): 635–652.

Bell, Derrick. "Racial Realism." *Connecticut Law Review 24*, (1992): 363–379.

Bennett, Pamela, Lutz, Amy, and Lakshmi Jayaram. "Beyond the Schoolyard: The Role of Parenting Logics, Financial Resources, and Social Institutions in the Social Class Gap." *Structured Activity Participation Sociology of Education* 85, No. 2 (2012): 131–157.

Block, Caryn, Aumann, Kerstin, and Amy Chelin. "Assessing Stereotypes of Black and White Managers: A Diagnostic Ratio Approach." *Journal Of Applied Social Psychology 42, (2012):* 128–149.

Bonanno, Alessandro and Goetz, Stephan. "Wal-Mart and Local Economic Development: A Survey." *Economic Development Quarterly* 26, no.4 (2012): 285–297.

Bonilla-Silva, Eduardo. *Racism Without Racists: Color-Blind Racism and the Persistence of Racial Inequality in America.* Lanham, MD: Rowman & Littlefield Publishers, 2013.

Booker, Kimberly and Mitchell, Angela. "Patterns in Recidivism and Discretionary Placement in Disciplinary Alternative Education: The Impact of Gender, Ethnicity, Age, and Special Education Status." *Education and Treatment of Children* 34, no. 2 (2011): 193–208.

Brettschneider, Alecia and Fred Shelley. "Examining Wal-Mart's Relationships with Local Communities through Investigation of Advertising," In *Wal-Mart World,* edited by Stanley Brunn, 193-202. New York: Taylor and Francis Group, 2006.

Brunsma, David, Brown, Eric, and Peggy Placier. "Teaching Race at Historically White Colleges and Universities: Identifying and Dismantling the Walls of Whiteness." *Critical Sociology 39,* no. 5 (2013): 717–738.

Bruenig, Matt. 2014. "White High School Dropouts Have More Wealth than Black and Hispanic College Graduates." *Policyshop.* September 23, 2014. Accessed September 27, 2014. http://www.demos.org/blog/9/23/14/white-high-school-dropouts-have-more-wealth-black-and-hispanic-college-graduates.

Buras, Kristen. "Race, Charter Schools, and Conscious Capitalism: On the Spatial Politics of Whiteness as Property (and the Unconscionable Assault on Black New Orleans," *Harvard Educational Review* 81, no. 2 (2011): 296–330.

Burd-Sharps, Sarah, Kristen Lewis, and Eduardo Borges Martin. *A Portrait of Louisiana: Louisiana Human Development Report.* American Human Development Project of the Social Sciences Research Council, 2009.

Caren, Neal. 2007. "Political Process Theory." In *Blackwell Encyclopedia of Sociology.* edited by George Ritzer. Boston: Wiley-Blackwell, 2007.

Castellanos, Dalina. "More Than 2 dozen LA Unified Magnet Schools Under-Enrolled." *Los Angeles Times.* October 23, 2012. Accessed September 28, 2014. http://articles.latimes.com/print/2012/oct/23/local/la-me-lausd-magnet-enroll-20121023.

"Children in Louisiana." *Children's Defense Fund.* Children's Defense Fund, Mar. 2013. Web. Mar. 2014.

Clark, Tom and Anthony Heath. *Hard Times: The Diverse Toll of the Economic Slump.* Hartford: Yale University Press, 2014.

Cline, Rodney. "Chapter 1." *Education in Louisiana: History and Development.* Baton Rouge, LA: Claitor's Pub. Division, 1974.

Cline, Rodney. "Chapter 4." *Education in Louisiana: History and Development.* Baton Rouge, LA: Claitor's Pub. Division, 1974.

Cody, Anthony. "The Common Core Equity Swindle." *Education Week.* Education Week, 10 Mar. 2014. Web. Mar. 2014.

Collins, Jane. "Wal-Mart, American Consumer Citizenship, and the 2008 Recession." *Focaal* 61, no. 1 (2011): 107–116.

Condron, Dennis. "Social class, school and non-school environments, and black/white inequalities in children's learning." *American Sociological Review* 74 no. 5 (2009): 685–708.

Courtemanche, Charles. "Supersizing Supercenters? The Impact of Wal-Mart Supercenters on Body Mass Index and Obesity." *Journal of Urban Economics* 69 no. 2 (2011): 165–181.

Crouter, Ann, Megan E. Baril; Kelly D. Davis; Susan M. McHale. "Processes Linking Social Class and Racial Socialization in African American Dual-Earner Families." *Journal of Marriage and Family* 70, No. 5 (2008): 1311–1325.

Curry, Tommy. "Saved by the Bell: Derrick Bell's Racial Realism as Pedagogy." *Ohio Valley Philosophy of Education Society 39* (2008): 35–46.

Dahlberg, Robin. *Locking Up Our Children: The Secure Detention of Massachusetts Youth After Arraignment and Before Adjudication.* Washington, DC: American Civil Liberty Union. 2008.

Dahlberg, Robin. *Arrested Futures: The Criminalization of School Discipline in Massachusetts' Three Largest School Districts.* Washington, DC: American Civil Liberty Union. 2012.

Davis, Tomeka. "School Choice and Segregation: Racial Equality in Magnet Schools." *Education and Urban Society* 46, no. 4 (2014): 399–433.

DeParle, Jason. "Broken Levees, Unbroken Barriers." *The New York Times.* The New York Times, September 3, 2005. Web. Mar. 2014.

Desilver, Drew. "Black Incomes Are Up, But Wealth Isn't" *Pew Research Center.* http://www.pewresearch.org/fact-tank/2013/08/30/black-incomes-are-up-but-wealth-isnt/. 2013.

Dewan, Shaila. "Mostly White Forces in Mostly Black Towns: Police Struggle for Racial Diversity." *New York Times.* http://www.nytimes.com/2014/09/10/us/for-small-police-departments-increasing-diversity-is-a-struggle.html?_r=0. 2014.

Diemer, Matthew, Mistry, Rashmita, Wadsworth, Martha, Lopez, Irene, and Faye Reimers. "Best Practices in Conceptualizing and Measuring Social Class in Psychological Research." *Analyses of Social Issues and Public Policy* 13, no. 1 (2013): 77–113.

Drew, Emily. "Listening Through White Ears: Cross-Racial Dialogues as a Strategy to Address the Racial Effects of Gentrification." *Journal of Urban Affairs* 34, no. 1 (2012): 99–115.

DuBois WEB. *Souls of Black Folks.* Chicago: A. C. McClurg & Co. 1903.

Eggler, Bruce. "Civil Rights Struggle Lives on in La.'s Public Schools." *NOLA.com.* The Times Picayune, July 28, 2007. Web. Mar. 2014.

el-Khoury, Laura. "Begin While Black: Resistance and the Management of the Self." *Social Identities* 18, no. 1 (2012): 85–100.

Ellickson, Paul and Grieco, Paul. 2013. "Wal-Mart and the Geography of Grocery Retailing." *Journal of Urban Economics.* 75 (2013): 1–4.

Epps, Edgar G. "Race, Class, and Educational Opportunity: Trends in the Sociology of Education." *Sociological Forum* 10, no. 4 (1995): 593–608.

Fasching-Varner, Kenneth, Mitchell, Roland, Martin, Lori and Karen P. Bennett-Haron. "Beyond School-to-Prison Pipeline and Toward an Educational and Penal Realism." *Equity & Excellence in Education* 47, no. 4 (2014): 410–429.

Feagin, Joe. *The White Racial Frame.* New York, NY: Routledge, 2010.

Frankenberg, Erica, and Genevieve Siegel-Hawley. 2008. "The Forgotten Choice? Rethinking Magnet Schools in a Changing Landscape." *The Civil Rights Project.* http://civilrightsproject.ucla.edu/research/k-12-education/integration-and-diversity/the-forgotten-choice-rethinking-magnet-schools-in-a-changing-landscape/frankenberg-forgotten-choice-rethinking-magnet.pdf.

Franklin, Robert. *Crisis in the Village.* Minneapolis: Fortress Press, 2007.

Gaidimas, Linda and Susan Walters. "Maine's Common Core of Learning Moves Forward." *Educational Leadership* 50, no. 8 (1993): 31–34.

Glandon, P.J. and Jaremski, Matthew. "Sales and Firm Entry: The Case of Wal-Mart." *Southern Economic Journal* 81, no. 1 (2014): 168–192.

Goetz, Stephen and Anil Rupasingha. "Social Capital, Religion, Wal-Mart and Hate Groups in America." *Social Science Quarterly* 93 no. 2 (2012): 379.

Green, Gary Paul and Anna Haines. *Asset Building & Community Development.* Los Angeles: Sage, 2012.

Green, Richard. "Plutocracy, Bureaucracy, and the End of Public Trust." *Administration & Society* 44, no. 1 (2012): 109–143.

Griswold, Allison. "The American Concept of 'Prestige' Has Barely Changed in 37 Years." *Slate.* (September 10, 2014). Accessed September 27. http://www.slate.com/blogs/moneybox/2014/09/10/most_prestigious_jobs_in_america_the_short_list_has_barely_changed_in_37.html.

Gregory, Ann and Rhonda Weinstein. "The Discipline Gap and African Americans: Defiance or Cooperation in the High School Classroom." *Journal of School Psychology* 46 (2008): 455–475.

Grogger, Jeffrey. "The Effects of Civil Gang Injunctions on Reported Violent Crime: Evidence from Los Angeles County." *Journal of Law and Economics* XLV, (2012): 69–91.

Hacker, Andrew. *Two Nations: Black and White, Separate, Hostile, Unequal.* New York: Scribner's, 1992.

Hacker, Andrew, and Claudia Dreifus. "Who's Minding the Schools?" *The New York Times.* The New York Times, June 8, 2013. Web. Mar. 2014.

Hall, Leda and Hall, Melvin. "A Growth Machine for Those Who County." *Critical Sociology* 20, (1994): 79–101.

Hanauer, Nick. 2012. "A Message from Us Rich Plutocrats to All You Little People." *Business Insider.* http://www.businessinsider.com/a-message-from-us-rich-plutocrats-to-all-you-little-people-2012-11.

Harcourt, Bernard. "Reflecting on the Subject: A Critique of the Social Influence Conception of Deterrence, The Broken Windows Theory, and Order-Maintenance Policing New York Style." *Michigan Law Review* 97, no. 2 (1998): 291.

Harris, Thomas. *The Story of Public Education in Louisiana.* Baton Rouge, Dissertation. 1924.

Harris-Perry, Melissa. 2011. "Breaking News: Not All Black Intellectuals Think Alike." *The Nation.*

"History of the Federal Judiciary." *History of the Federal Judiciary.* Federal Judicial Center, n.d. Web. Mar. 2014.

Horton, Hayward Derrick, Allen, Beverlyn, Herring, Cedric and Melvin Thomas. "Lost in the Storm: The Sociology of the Black Working-Class 1850 to 1990." *American Sociological Review* 65, no. 11 (2000): 128–137.

Horwitz, Steven. "Wal-Mart to the Rescue: Private Enterprise's Response to Hurricane Katrina." *Independent Review* 13, no. 4 (2009): 511–528.

Hwang, Jackelyn and Sampson, Robert. "Divergent Pathways of Gentrification." *American Sociological Review,* 79(4): 726–751.

Irvine, Jacqueline and Darlene York. "Teacher perspectives: Why do African-American, Hispanic, and Vietnamese students fail?" in *Handbook of Schooling in Urban America,* edited by Stanley Rothstein, 160–173. Westport: Greenwood Press, 1993.

Jacobs, Nicholas. 2013. "Understanding School Choice: Location as a Determinant of Charter School Racial, Economic, and Linguistic Segregation." *Education and Urban Society* 45, no. 4: 459–482.

Jimoh, Yemisi. "The Messenger (1917-1928)" 2005. http://works.bepress.com/jimoh/25.

Johnson, Karl. "Police-Black Community Relations in Postwar Philadelphia: Race and Criminalization in Urban Social Spaces, 1945-1960." *Journal of African American History* (2004): 118–134.

"Judge: Voucher Law, Tangipahoa Parish Desegregation Order Conflict." *American Press - Local.* American Press, November 26, 2012. Web. Mar. 2014.

Kanter, Rosebeth Moss. "Leadership for Change: Enduring Skills for Change Masters." *Harvard Business School* (2003): 1–16.

Kay Melchior, Jillian. "Lessons from Katrina." *National Review* 65.20 (2013): 40–43.

Kozol, Jonathan. *Savage Inequalities: Children in America's Schools.* New York, NY: Broadway Books, 1991.

Krieger, Nancy, Williams, David, and Nancy Moss. "Measuring Social Class in US Public Health Research: Concepts, Methodologies, and Guidelines." *Annual Review of Public Health* 18, (2007): 341–378.

Krugman, Paul. 2009. "How Did Economists Get It So Wrong." *New York Times.* http://www.nytimes.com/2009/09/06/magazine/06Economic-t.html?pagewanted=all&_r=0.

Lawler, Edward and Susan Mohman. "Quality Circles After the Fad." *Harvard Business Review* (1985): 65–71.

Lauren, Douglas Lee. "To Choose or Not to Choose: High School Choice and Graduation in Chicago." *Educational Evaluation and Policy Analysis* 31, no. 3 (2009): 179–199.

Layte, Richard and Christopher Whelan. "Explaining Social Class Inequalities in Smoking: The Role of Education, Self-Efficacy, and Deprivation." *European Sociological Review* 25, no. 4 (2009): 399–410.

"Lawsuit Aims to Curb L.A.'s Use of Gang Injunction Curfews." *Daily Breeze.* (September 13, 2013). http://www.dailybreeze.com/general-news/20130914/lawsuit-aims-to-curb-las-use-of-gang-injunction-curfews.

Leeland, Chrystia. *Plutocrats: The Rise of New Global Super-Rich and the Fall of Everyone Else.* New York: Penguin Books, 2012.

Lewis, Kristine and Stephanie McKissic. "American Students Participation in the Black Campus Community as an Act of Resistance." *Journal of Black Studies* 41, no. 2 (2010: 264–280.

Littler, Jo. "Meritocracy as Plutocracy: The Marketing of 'Equality' Under Neoliberalism." *New Formations* (2013): 52–72.

Liu, Goodwin, and William L. Taylor. 2005. *"School Choice to Achieve Desegregation." Fordham Law Review* 74 (2005): 791. http://ir.lawnet.fordham.edu/flr/vol74/iss2/16.

Logan, John. "The Mounting Guerilla War Against the Reign of Wal-Mart." *Forum* 23, no.1 (2013): 22–29.

Logan, John, and Harvey Molotch. *Urban Fortunes: The Political Economy of Place.* Berkeley: University of California Press, 1987.

Louisiana: "Demographics of Poor Children." *NCCP.* National Center for Children in Poverty, n.d. Web. Mar. 2014.

Louisiana| KIDS COUNT Data Center." *Louisiana| KIDS COUNT Data Center.* Annie E Casey Foundation/Kids Count, n.d. Web. Mar. 2014.

Lutz, Ashley. "These Six Corporations Control 90 Percent of the Media in America." *Business Insider.* http://www.businessinsider.com/these-6-corporations-control-90-of-the-media-in-america-2012-6, 2012.

Madrick, Jeff. "Ted Turner, Sam Walton, and Steve Ross." In *Age of Greed,* edited by Jeff Madrick, 125–143. Knopf: New York, 2011.

Martin, Lori Latrice. *Black Asset Poverty and the Enduring Racial Divide.* Boulder, CO: First Forum Press, 2013.

Martinez, Michael, Banchero, Stephanie, and Darnell Little. "Race, Poverty, Define Failing Schools." *Chicago Tribune.* Retrieved from http://articles.chicagotribune.com/2002-07-21/news/0207210275_1_magnet-schools-private-schools-public-schools.

Matthews, Dylan. "A $15 Minimum Wage is a Bad Idea." *Washington Post.* http://www.washingtonpost.com/blogs/wonkblog/wp/2013/06/22/a-15-minimum-wage-is-a-terrible-idea/, 2013.

Massengill, Rebekah. "Why Evangelicals Like Wal-Mart: Education, Region, and Religious Group Identity." *Sociology of Religion* 72, no.1 (2011): 50–77.

McCarthy, John D. and Mayer N. Zald. "Resource Mobilization and Social Movements: A Partial Theory." *The American Journal of Sociology* 82, no. 6 (1977): 1212–1241.

McKernan, Signe-Mary, Ratcliffe, Caroline, Steuerle, Eugene, and Sisi Zhang. *Less than Equal: Racial Disparities in Wealth Accumulation.* New York, NY: Urban Institute, 2013.

McNichol, Elizabeth, Douglas Hall, David Cooper, and Vincent Palacios. "Center on Budget and Policy Priorities."*Pulling Apart: A State-by-State Analysis of Income Trends —.* N. p., November, 15 2012. Web. Mar. 2014.

Mitchell, Gail. 2013. "Fewer and Fewer African American Owned Radio Stations Reports Show." http://www.billboard.com/biz/articles/news/1539311/fewer-and-fewer-african-american-owned-radio-stations-reports-show.

Mistler, Steve. "Virtual Charter School 'With Striking Distance' of Enrollment Benchmark." *Portland Press Herald.* July 1, 2014. Retrieved September 28, 2014. http://www.pressherald.com/2014/07/01/maine-charter-school-commission-virtual-charter-school-within-striking-distance-of-enrollment-benchmark/.

Molotch, Harvey. "The Political Economy of Growth Machines." *Journal of Urban Affairs* 15, no. 1 (1993): 29–53.

Molotch, Harvey. "The City as a Growth Machine: Toward a Political Economy of Place." *American Journal of Sociology* 82, no. 2 (1976): 309–332.

Monnat, Shannon. The Color of Welfare Sanctioning: Exploring the Individual and Contextual Roles of Race on TANF Case Closures and Benefit Reductions." *Sociological Quarterly 51,* n. 4 (2010): 678–707.

Moreno, Paul. Black Americans and Organized Labor: A New History. Baton Rouge: Louisiana State University Press, 2006.

Mukherjee, Elora and Martin Karpatkin. *Criminalizing the Classroom: The Over-Policing of New York City Schools.* New York Civil Liberty Union, 2007.

Muniz, Ana. "Maintaining Racial Boundaries: Criminalization, Neighborhood Context, and the Origins of Gang Injunctions." *Social Problems* 61, no. 2 (2014): 216–236.

Naison, Mark. October 22, 2013. "The Making of an Education Catastrophe-One Activist's Journey of Discovery. Retrieved from http://withabrooklynaccent.blogspot.com/2013/10/ted-x-talk-my-journey-to-education.html on November 22, 2014.

New York Civil Liberties Union. "Look at School Discipline: Zero Tolerance Discipline, Discrimination, and the School to Prison Pipeline." http://www.nyclu.org/schoolprison.

Pew Research Center. "Wal-Mart a good Place to Shop But Some Critics Too." http://www.people-press.org/2005/12/15/wal-mart-a-good-place-to-shop-but-some-critics-too/2/, 2005.

Polleta, Francesca and James M. Jasper. 2001. "Collective Identity and Social Movements." *Annual Review of Sociology.* 27, (2001): 283–305.

Pownall, Samantha. "A, B, C, D, STPP: How School Discipline Feeds the School-to-Prison Pipeline." New York Civil Liberties Union, 2013.

National Center for Education Statistics. 2010. "Median annual earnings for full-time, full-year wage and salary workers ages 25 and older, by educational attainment, sex, and race/ethnicity: 2007." http://ncces.ed.gov/pub2010/2010015/tables/table_29.asp.

National Center for Education Statistics. 2010. "Percentage distribution of adults ages 25 and over according to highest level of educational attainment, by race/ethnicity: Selected years, 1996–2008.)" http://ncces.ed.gov/pub2010/2010015/tables/table_27a.asp.

National Center for Education Statistics. 2010. "Percentage of children ages 6 to 18, by parent's highest level of educational attainment and child's race/ethnicity: 2008." http://ncces.ed.gov/pub2010/2010015/tables/table_5.asp.

National Center for Education Statistics. 2010. "Unemployment rates for persons ages 16 years and older, by educational attainment, age group, and race/ethnicity: 2008." http://ncces.ed.gov/pub2010/2010015/tables/table_28.asp.

National Commission on Excellence in Education. 1983. "A Nation at Risk: The Imperative for Educational Reform."

National Public Radio. "The Common Core FAQ." May 27, 2014.

National Public Radio. 2012. "A Startling Gap Between Us and Them In 'Plutocrats." http://www.npr.org/templates/transcript/transcript.php?storyId=162799512.

Onwuachi-Willig, Angela. "Celebrating Critical Race Theory at 20." *Iowa Law Review* 94 (2009): 1497–1504.

Ott, Lesli. "Big-Box Retail and Its Impact on Local Communities." *Liber8* (2008). Retrieved September 29, 2014. https://research.stlouisfed.org/pageone-economics/uploads/newsletter/2008/200801.pdf.

Poverty Rate by Race/Ethnicity "The Henry J. Kaiser Family Foundation." *Poverty Rate by Race/Ethnicity.* Kaiser Family Foundation, n.d. Web. Mar. 2014.

Public Affairs Research Council of Louisiana, Inc. *Improving Quality during School Desegregation.* Baton Rouge: n.p., 1969. Print.

"Quality Circle." *The Economist.* November 4, 2009.

Ravitch, Diane. "Speech to Modern Language Association." January 11, 2014

Rich, Motoko. "School Standards' Debut Is Rocky, and Critics Pounce." *The New York Times.* August 15, 2013. Web. March 2014.

Rich, Motoko. "School Data Finds Pattern of Inequality Along Racial Lines." *The New York Times,* March 20, 2014. Web. March 2014.

Riley, Chloe. "Whitney Young Film to Show Stress, Joy of School's Students and Applicants." *DNA Info Chicago.* April 16, 2014. Retrieved September 28. http://www.dnainfo.com/chicago/20140416/near-west-side/whitney-young-film-show-stress-joy-of-schools-students-applicants.

Ritzer, George. *The McDonaldization of Society.* Los Angeles, CA: Sage, 2007.

Sachs, Jeffrey. "Understanding and Overcoming America's Plutocracy." *Huffington Post* (2014).

Samuels, Diana. "St. George, La.: One Group's Quest for a New City Could Determine the Fate of Metropolitan Baton Rouge." *NOLA.com*. The Times Picayune, November 19, 2013. Web. Mar. 2014.

Samuels, Diana. "Sen. Mack 'Bodi' White Pre-filing Bill to Restructure East Baton Rouge School System." *NOLA.com*. The Times Picayune, Feb. 28, 2014. Web. Mar. 2014.

Schwadel, Philip. "Social Class and Finding a Congregation: How Attendees are Introduced to Their Congregations." *Review of Religious Research* 54, no. 4 (2012): 543–554.

"Parents in Prison." Washington, DC: The Sentencing Project, 2012.

Shin, Naomi and Richardo Otheguy. "Social Class and Gender Impacting Change in Bilingual Settings: Spanish Subject Pronoun Use in New York." *Language in Society* 42, no. 4 (2013): 429–452.

Shiner, Max. *Civil Gang Injunctions: A Guide for Prosecutors*. Washington, DC: Bureau of Justice Assistance. 2009.

Singer, Alan. "Uncommon Core Heightens Race and Class Math Divide." *The Huffington Post*. March 10, 2014. Web. Mar. 2014.

Skiba, Russell, Horner, Robert, Chung, Choong-Geun, Rausch, M.Karega, May, Seth, and Tary Tobin. "Race is Not Neutral: A National Investigation of African American and Latino Disproportionately in School Discipline." *School Psychological Review* 40, no. 1 (2011): 85–107.

Souris Theodore. Stop and Frisk or Arrest and Search: The Use and Misuse of Euphemisms. *The Journal of Criminal Law, Criminology and Police Science* 57, no. 3 (1966): 251–264.

Springer, Kristen and Mouzon, Dawne. "'Macho Men' and Preventive Health Care: Implications for Older Men in Different Social Classes." *Journal of Health and Social Behavior* 52, no. 2 (2011): 212–227.

Strauss, Valerie. "A Dozen Problems with Charter Schools." *Washington Post*. May 20, 2014. Retrieved September 28, 2014. http://www.washingtonpost.com/blogs/answer-sheet/wp/2014/05/20/a-dozen-problems-with-charter-schools/.

Tate, Gayle. "Free Black Resistance in the Antebellum Era, 1830 to 1860." *Journal of Black Studies*, 28, no. 6 (1998): 764–782.

Taylor, Henry. "Are Community Schools Effective Pathways Out of Poverty: A Commentary by Henry Louis Taylor, Jr." National Symposium on Community Schools as Vehicles for School and Community Revitalization: Rebuilding Social Capital through Community Schools and the Role of Higher Education." The Center for Community Partnerships, University of Pennsylvania, Philadelphia, Pennsylvania, 2005. Retrieved from http://www.centerforurbanstudies.com/documents/urban_education/reframing_the_community_school_debate.pdf on November 22, 2014.

Taylor, Henry and Linda McGlynn. (2010). "The Community as Classroom Initiative: The Case of Futures Academy in Buffalo, New York." *University and Community Schools* 8, no. 1–2 (2010): 31–44.

Thompson, Krissah. "Cornel West's Criticism of Obama Sparks Debate among African Americans." *The Washington Post*. 2011.

Twine, France Winddance. "Feminist Fairy Tales for Black and American Indian Girls: A Working-Class Vision." *Signs* 25, no. 4 (2000): 1227–1230.

United States Department of Agriculture—Household Food Security in the United States in 2012." *USDA ERS—Household Food Security in the United States in 2012*. United States Department of Agriculture, n.d. Web. 2014.

United States Department of Education. National Center for Education Statistics. 2013a.

United States Department of Education. National Center for Education Statistics *The Conditions of Education*. NCES 2009-081, Table A-32-1, Washington, D.C.: United States Government Printing Office, 2009.

United States Department of Education. National Center for Education Statistics. *Characteristics of Public, Private, and Bureau of Indian Education Elementary and Secondary Schools in the United States: Results from the 2007-08 Schools and Staffing Survey*. NCES 2009-321. Washington, D.C.: United States Government Printing Office, 2009b.

United States Department of Education, National Center for Education Statistics. *Percentage of high school dropouts among persons 16 through 24 (status dropout rate), by sex and race/ ethnicity: Selected years, 1960 through 2012.* NCES 2013. Table 219.70, Washington, D.C.: United States Government Printing Office, 2013c.

United States Department of Education, National Center for Education Statistics. *Public School Graduates and Dropouts from the Common Core Data: School Year 2009–10.* NCES 2013-309. Washington, D.C.:U.S. United States Government Printing Office, 2013d.

U.S. Department of Education Office for Civil Rights. Civil Rights Data Collection. Data Snapshot: School Discipline. www2.ed.gov/about/offices/list/ocr/docs/crdcdiscipline-snap-shop.pdf.

Van Riber, Thomas. 2006. "America's Most Admired Professions." *Forbes.* July 28, 2014. http://www.forbes.com/2006/07/28/leadership-careers-jobs-cx_tvr_0728admired.html.

Walton, Sam. 1992. *Made in America: My Story.* NY: Double Day, 1992.

Walsh, Eileen, Torr, Berna, and Ha Bui Bonnie. Inequalities in Self-Rated Health: Untangling Ethnicity, Social Class, and Lifestyle Effects on the Vietnamese, other Asians, Hispanics, and Whites." *International Review of Modern Sociology* 36, no. 2 (2010): 195–220.

Ward, Steven. "Report: Poverty High in Baton Rouge." *Report: Poverty High in Baton Rouge.* The Advocate, November 3, 2011. Web. Mar. 2014.

Washington, Rodney, Tenette Smith, Brenda Jones, and Henry Robinson. "Hurricane Katrina Three Years Later: Implications of Race, Poverty, and Equity on the Restructuring of the New Orleans Public School System." *Researcher: An Interdisciplinary Journal* 22, no. 1 (2008): 1–22.

Weathersbee, Tonya. "Black Dropout Rate Remains Too High." *The Florida Times Union.* October 18, 2012. Retrieved September 27, 2014 http://jacksonville.com/opinion/blog/ 403605/tonyaa-weathersbee/2012-10-18/tonyaa-weathersbee-black-dropout-rate-remains-too.

Weber, Max. *The Theory of Social and Economic Organization.* New York: Oxford University Press, 1947.

Weis, Lois and Julia Hall. "I Had a Lot of Black Friends Growing up that my Father Didn't Know About." *Journal of Gender Studies.* 10, no. 1 (2001): 43–66.

Wheary, Jennifer, Shapiro, Thomas, Tamara Draut, Tatjana Meschede. *Economic (In)Security: The Experience of the African American and Latino Middle Classes.* 2008.

Wilson, William J. *The Declining Significance of Race.* Chicago: University of Chicago Press, 1979.

Wilson, William Julius. "The Declining Significance of Race: Revisited & Revised." *Daedalus* 140, no. 2 (2011): 55–69.

Wolfe, Scott E. and David C. Pyrooz. "Rolling Back Prices and Raising Crime Rates? The Wal-Mart Effect on Crime in the United States." *British Journal of Criminology* 54, no. 2: (2014): 199–221.

Wollan, Malia. "Gang Injunction Names Names, and Suit Follows." *The New York Times.* 2010.

Young, Justin and Charlie Potter. "Trail or Dog: The Common Core Standards, Philanthrocapi-talism, and the Future of Higher Education." *Ethos: A Digital Review of Arts, Humanities, and Public Ethnics* 1, no. 2 (2014): 49–71.

Zeitlin, Maurice, and L. Frank Weyher. "'Black and White, Unite and Fight': Interracial Work-ing-Class Solidarity and Racial Employment Equality." *American Journal of Sociology* 107, (2001): 430–67.

Index

About the Author

Dr. **Lori Latrice Martin** is an associate professor of sociology and African and African American Studies at Louisiana State University. Dr. Martin is the author of numerous academic journal articles and books. Her most recent publications include: *Black Asset Poverty and the Enduring Racial Divide, The Ex-Slave's Fortune: The Story of Cynthia D. Hesdra, Out of Bounds: Racism and the Black Athlete, White Sports/Black Sports: Racial Disparities in Athletic Programs,* and *Trayvon Martin, Race, and American Justice: Writing Wrong.* Dr. Martin holds a doctorate in sociology from the University at Albany, State University of New York.

CPSIA information can be obtained at www.ICGtesting.com
Printed in the USA
BVOW05*0746100415

395552BV00002B/4/P